"Want to know how to write alien creature dialog? Want to ~~cook~~ up convincing futures? Want to know the difference between sci-fi and fantasy? Look no further. Robert Grant takes you on a fascinating journey through cinematic otherworlds, showing how the genre has changed over the years while remaining one of the most popular with movie audiences. His smart, no-nonsense story tips are just as applicable to general screenwriting. *Writing the Science Fiction Film* is concise, illuminating, and simply a swell read, whether you want to write sci-fi or just watch it."

— Joe Dante, director: *Gremlins, Explorers, Innerspace*

"This is the book I never quite got around to writing, but done with far more eloquence and knowledge. If you want to write sci-fi, this is the perfect place to start."

— Chris Patmore, *MovieScope* magazine, author: *Movie Making Course: The Ultimate Guide for the Aspiring Filmmaker*

"*Writing the Science Fiction Film* breaks down tried and true techniques of crafting a science fiction film. But what I really like about the book are the exercises at the end of various sections and some very nice brainstorming drills that are generally useful for all forms of writing, but certainly for sci-fi. A great read for anyone getting into the genre."

— Nathyn Brendan Masters, filmmaker: *The 4th Beast*; author: *The Action Filmmaking Workbook*

"Robert Grant's *Writing the Science Fiction Film* is a must-have for anyone writing a genre-inspired screenplay. His guidelines and advice are excellent tools at helping the writer organize the rules and the mythology of their created universe without getting bogged down. There's also plenty of fantastic guidelines on additional tropes, including sidekicks, creating aliens, brainstorming and most importantly, applying real science and fake science seamlessly into one's screenplay."

— Stefan Blitz, editor-in-chief, Forcesofgeek.com

"Robert Grant's *Writing the Science Fiction Film* is about the process of crafting great science fiction stories like the ones we've grown to love. A great journey through the best in science fiction movies and television, and a great resource for any writer interested in crafting their own science fiction stories."
— Tom Farr, Tom Farr Reviews

"If you need, like me, to work with wild robots, cannibal mutants, or creatures from outer space, this wonderful book isn't only useful, but indispensable!"
— Marc Caro, writer/director: *The City of Lost Children, Delicatessen*

"Oh, what a joy this book is! First of all, it does all the right things: supplies excellent information and instruction. Background and future possibilities are covered, not only in the genre, but in your writing. But best of all, it's a darned interesting and entertaining read. Absolutely love it!
— Sable Jak, author: *Writing The Fantasy Film, Heroes and Journeys in Alternate Realities*

WRITING THE
SCIENCE
FICTION FILM

ROBERT GRANT

Published by Michael Wiese Productions
12400 Ventura Blvd. #1111
Studio City, CA 91604
tel. 818.379.8799
fax 818.986.3408
mw@mwp.com
www.mwp.com

Cover design: Johnny Ink www.johnnyink.com
Book interior design: Gina Mansfield Design
Copy editor: Matt Barber

Printed by McNaughton & Gunn, Inc., Saline, Michigan
Manufactured in the United States of America

Library of Congress Cataloging-in-Publication Data

Grant, Robert, 1962-
Writing the science fiction film / Robert Grant.
    pages cm
ISBN 978-1-61593-136-1
1. Science fiction films--Authorship. 2. Motion picture authorship--Hand-
books, manuals, etc. I. Title.
PN1995.9.S26G83 2013
808.2'3--dc23
                            2013002979

Printed on recycled stock.
Publisher plants 10 trees for every one tree used to produce this book.

MIX
Paper
FSC FSC® C011935

~

For Helen, Callum, and Jessica;
My whole universe.

~

CONTENTS

ACKNOWLEDGEMENTS

As you get older you understand the truth that you are the sum total of everyone you've met and everything you've experienced, everything you've read and everything you've watched, and everything you've been taught up to that point. Thus it is an impossible task to thank all those thousands of people you've come across along the way, and who have had some influence on you, however fleeting.

But here goes.

I have to start with my Mum and Dad, who taught me to read, and gave me books, and instilled in me a lifelong love of storytelling in all its forms for which I will always be grateful. Thank you.

I have to say a special thank you to my friend Louis Savy, Festival Director of SCI-FI-LONDON, font of all knowledge, quizmaster extraordinaire, and walking, talking IMDb for science fiction film. How on Earth do you remember all that stuff? I'd also like to give a shout out to the core SFL team and to the many volunteers who, over the years, have made the SCI-FI-LONDON Film Festival such a success and such amazing fun to be a part of.

I'd like to say "Hi!" to the small band of the South Bank Screenwriters Group — you know who you are — I've cherished the arguments and anecdotes that we've shared over the years; long may the drinking and dreaming continue.

A big thank you has to go to Ken Lee, Michael Wiese, and everyone at Michael Wiese Productions for the opportunity to write this book and the encouragement and patience in putting it together.

And finally, it would be remiss of me to not acknowledge a huge thanks to all of the screenwriters, directors, actors, and crewmembers of all the great (and not so great) science fiction films I've loved watching over the years, and to the many, many science fiction writers whose books I enjoyed from such an early age, and continue to enjoy to this day. You have all been a huge influence on me and I thank you for that. I also owe a debt of gratitude to the teachers whose classes I've attended and books I've read over many years of studying the craft. Having learned something useful from every one of you, I am truly standing on the shoulders of giants.

Robert

INTRODUCTION

I guess it really starts with my Mum. She taught me to read long before I reached school age, and it was through her, probably when I was around six, that I came into possession of my first science fiction novel — *Tom Swift and The Mystery Comet*. Not exactly a landmark work within the genre admittedly, but at such an impressionable age the idea of UFOs, strange comets, Brungarian spies, and the Telesampler launched my imagination skyward, opening the floodgates for a reading habit that hasn't waned to this day. Other books quickly followed, more of Tom Swift, but also the classics, Jules

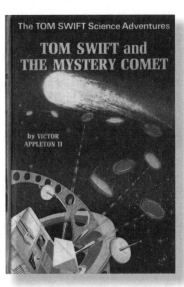

The TOM SWIFT Science Adventures
TOM SWIFT and THE MYSTERY COMET
by VICTOR APPLETON II

Where, for me, it all began.

Verne and H.G. Wells, until I traded up and discovered Robert Heinlein and Edgar Rice Burroughs, Isaac Asimov and Arthur C. Clarke. Then there was TV: *Dr. Who*, *Fireball XL5*, *Lost in Space*, *Thunderbirds*, even *The Jetsons*, and of course, *Star Trek*. Science fiction had called out to me and I was ready and eager to listen.

But then the world changed forever.

On July 21, 1969, at 02:56 GMT, Neil Armstrong cemented his place in history with the immortal words "That's one small step for man, one giant leap for mankind" — and for this small boy in London, staring wide-eyed at the grainy black and white images being transmitted from the surface of the moon, all my dreams had come true. Because from where I sat, a foot from the screen, arms wrapped around my knees, I was watching the future.

Suddenly it was all so real, TV was full of space exploration. There was speculation about alien life, about the possibilities of living on the lunar surface, about the next flight, and the one after that, and when we'd reach Mars, and I drank it all in. Then the fruits of the research started to appear. Fischer space pens and Teflon non-stick saucepans were the tip of the iceberg. The real riches lay in tiny integrated circuits, satellite technology, GPS navigation systems, medical imaging equipment, miniaturised heart pumps, and water and air filtration systems. Fact is, we're still benefitting from that giant leap for mankind today.

I made my mind up early on that I was destined to be an astronaut. I was going to ride the crest of this wave of space enthusiasm to infinity and beyond — after all, I had the right stuff. Needless to say I soon came down to Earth with a bump, but it's probably no coincidence that I was front and centre when the first home computers came around, that I can remember being online *before* there was a "World Wide Web" and that I've spent almost 20 years designing user interfaces for software, websites, and mobile apps.

And at the heart of it all has been my love of this genre. Science fiction has surprised, aggravated, delighted, and infuriated me in equal measure, but above all it has always inspired me. I'm proud to be part of the core team that for the last 12 years has put on The London International Festival of Science Fiction and Fantastic Film — or SCI-FI-LONDON, as we like to be known — still the UK capital's only dedicated science fiction film festival. I'm also currently on the jury for The Arthur C. Clarke Award for Science Fiction Literature which, given where I started, is a tremendous honour, and I still have that copy of *Tom Swift and The Mystery Comet* (the cover you see is a scan of my copy). I still smile at the memories it evokes when I see it in my library, and that's really where this book comes in.

This is my chance to share my love of science fiction with the rest of the world. If you're reading this, you've already made up your mind that you're interested in writing science fiction screenplays, and why wouldn't you be? Take a look at the IMDb list of All-Time Box Office takings for the USA. Of the 523 films listed, more than 100 are pure science fiction. That doesn't include the *Lord of the Rings* trilogy or the eight *Harry Potter* films (which are fantasy movies anyway) and it also doesn't include the *Batman* films (which straddle a grey line between science fiction and fantasy) or the last *Indiana Jones* film (which is best forgotten) or a number of other "maybe" films that simply owe a debt to science fiction, because if I did there's probably a further 30 to add to that list. One way or another, science fiction is big business. Just ask Will Smith.

Will Smith celebrates another sci-fi hit. *(Independence Day, 1996)*

When Smith was plotting out the trajectory for his career, he took a look at which films consistently made money and he knew instantly that it had to be science fiction, and it worked! Take a look:

- *Independence Day*   (1996) $306,124,059
- *Men in Black*   (1997) $250,147,615
- *Men in Black II*   (2002) $190,418,803
- *I, Robot*   (2004) $144,795,350
- *I Am Legend*   (2007) $256,386,216
- *Hancock*   (2008) $227,946,274
- *Men in Black 3*   (2012) $174,787,898

That's a grand total of more than one and a half *billion* in box office dollars, and that's just in the USA alone! Okay, so obviously it helps that he's a decent actor, he's likeable and he's clearly a fan of the genre, but hell, science fiction has been so successful for Will Smith that even *Wild Wild West* (1999) made $113,745,408 at the U.S. box office, with its only claim to fame being a giant mechanical spider!

(Kind of Steampunk, if you were wondering... more on that later.) And if that doesn't convince you, take a look at Keanu Reeves' résumé. He's another go-to guy for science fiction, having done everything from comedy in the *Bill & Ted* films, to action in *The Matrix* trilogy, romance in *The Lake House*, noir-Cyberpunk in *Johnny Mnemonic*, pure science fiction drama in *The Day the Earth Stood Still*, and an out-there druggy cop story with *A Scanner Darkly*, and along the way he's also notched up well over a billion dollars in U.S. box office.

So science fiction sells, and it sells well, and right now there's never been a better time to be a science fiction screenwriter. TV is always filled with shows that have science fiction at their heart. *Warehouse 13, A Town Called Eureka, Alcatraz, Fringe, Primeval, Smallville, Battlestar Galactica, Heroes, Terra Nova, Firefly, The 4400, Terminator: The Sarah Connor Chronicles, Dollhouse, Lost, The X-Files* — the list is endless, and while not all of them last as long as they should (I'm looking at you, Fox!), the audience appetite is always there and the demand for new shows is stronger than ever. As I write this, the upcoming schedules are promising: *Person of Interest, Revolution, Touch, Awake, Arrow, The Neighbors, Zero Hour*, and animated series in the shape of *The Green Lantern, Adventure Time*, and *Tron Uprising*.

But science fiction doesn't always have to mean "big budget," and one of the key things I hope to impart in these pages is that you can write great science fiction — some of the best science fiction, in fact — without ever leaving our planet. For every *Avatar* there's an *Ever Since The World Ended*, for every *Transformers* there's a *Monsters*, and for every *Armageddon* there's an *Attack the Block*. Earth-bound stories, beautifully told, which means that YOU can be a part of it. You can write a science fiction story that's easy and cheap to make. You can pick up a DSLR camera and with a small crew of friends can get out there and start making films. Maybe short films to start, but as your skills grow and your confidence grows, so will your ambition and pretty soon it'll be your science fiction feature that we're premiering at SCI-FI-LONDON. I hope so, and I'll see you in the front row!

Cheers!
Robert Grant

How To Use This Book

This book has been put together as a guide to help you write better science fiction. It'll introduce you to the genre, explain the various kinds of science fiction stories, and then go through every stage of writing, from finding good ideas to developing characters, building science fiction worlds, getting the science right, perfecting dialogue, and finally, thinking about what to do beyond the writing and how you might go about making your own feature film.

If you've ever read a screenwriting book before or taken a screenwriting class, then the odds are good that some of what you read here, about character and dialogue, for instance, will be familiar to you, albeit this time framed within a science fiction context. The rest will hopefully be new to you, and my fervent wish is that it will open a doorway for you into the most fascinating, thought-provoking, and compelling genre in which to tell stories.

While I'd encourage you to make a first pass at this book by reading it through, it's probably not going to be necessary for everyone. If you're already familiar with the genre and have some screenwriting experience, you might want to skip straight to the chapters on worldbuilding or on getting the science right, although a refresher is always worth the time it takes to read. If you're new to the genre, then I would definitely start at the beginning by getting to understand what science fiction is, what compels writers to pick science fiction as the genre to write in, and why some stories lend themselves to science fiction perfectly and others do not. Beyond that I expect this book will be of most use if you keep it next to you and dip in and out of it from time to time while you write, using it as a reference book for when you've hit a rut in your story and you need a guideline to help pull you out of it.

But while the goal here is to get you to think a bit harder about the worlds you build and the science behind them, to make them more credible, more coherent, and more cohesive in ways that will stand up to scrutiny by even the most rabid science fiction fan, ultimately your first allegiance has to always be to the story. Audiences — including me — will forgive quite a lot of bad science and expository dialogue if the story hooks us in, makes us think a little about ourselves and our place in the universe, and ultimately carries us away on a great adventure.

So don't be a slave to the science and definitely don't try to write a science paper. Audiences are intelligent, and they want to be treated as such. But audiences want to be entertained above all else, so only write as much as is needed in order that things make sense, feel real, and keep us glued to the screen. We'll thank you for it.

CHAPTER ONE

WHAT IS SCIENCE FICTION?

THE DIFFERENCE BETWEEN SCIENCE FICTION AND FANTASY

"What is science fiction?" is a question that's been debated since the idea of "genre" has been around, and it's never really been satisfactorily answered. It's a bit like being asked "What is good taste?" It's kind of hard to pin down, but you'll know it when you see it. I mean, it's easy when you're watching a film with spaceships or aliens in it to point at the screen and say "Now that's sci-fi." But really, we both know there's a whole lot more to science fiction than the obvious tropes.

Whenever this question comes up I always say that the clue is in the name. It's SCIENCE fiction. That means that the story must absolutely rely on science in order to be told, and if it doesn't, then it's probably fantasy. Now that doesn't mean that the science in the story has to be real. Neither does it have to make sense (except within the logical parameters of its own world, and we'll get to that later). And it doesn't have to be set in the future, so I'm not necessarily talking about robots or spacecraft or "phasers on stun." But the science does have to be one of the major driving forces of the story. Without the science, the story could not be told.

A great example of this is *Back to the Future*. In the film, Doc Brown (Christopher Lloyd) converts a DeLorean automobile into a time machine using plutonium that he stole from Libyan terrorists. In order for time travel to happen, he has to deliver 1.21 gigawatts of electricity, directly into the Flux Capacitor, at the exact moment that the car hits 88mph, and *presto!* — the car will travel through time. Later, when Marty McFly (Michael J. Fox) is trapped in 1955, the only way to get back to 1985 is to use Doc Brown's converted DeLorean. Trouble is he doesn't have any plutonium and the only thing capable of generating that kind of power is a bolt of lightning. Luckily, Marty knows

1

exactly when and where the next lightning strike will happen, so Doc rigs up the car with a conducting rod so that, as long as Marty hits his mark at exactly the moment, while doing exactly 88mph, the lightning will send 1.21 gigawatts of electricity directly into the Flux Capacitor, sending Marty "back to the future."

Doc Brown (Christopher Lloyd) and Marty McFly (Michael J. Fox) get ready to see some serious shit. (*Back to the Future*, 1985)

This is classic science fiction. The story absolutely relies on the science to work. Without the science, the story could not be told. The fact that the science is utter nonsense is, of course, neither here nor there, and if you stopped to examine it in detail you'd be able to pull the whole thing apart in seconds, but actually what does matter is that the science is utterly consistent within the confines of the film and in both time periods. The physics (!) dictates 1.21 gigawatts of power into the Flux Capacitor at 88mph and the same is true in both 1985 and in 1955. The challenge is in harnessing that kind of power in 1955 to get Marty home and that is what makes *Back to the Future* such a terrific film. Remember, ultimately no one cares about the science. What they want to know is "Will Marty make it back before he ceases to exist, and what will the world be like when he gets there?"

— because like all great science fiction, the science drives the story, but it's the people we care about.

Let's look at an example of the flip side of this. When science fiction fans are trying to persuade folks who claim they don't like the genre, that actually they do and they just don't know it, they'll cite a film like *Sliding Doors*. Well I've got news for you guys, *Sliding Doors* isn't science fiction at all. Now at this point they'll start rambling on about parallel worlds and the story existing in two spaces simultaneously, but they're kidding themselves. There are no parallel worlds in *Sliding Doors*. Believe me, I've looked for them. What we actually have is a story about how one young woman's life might have been completely different if it weren't for some random event like catching a tube train. What we actually see is a fantasy that says maybe this could happen, or perhaps that might happen, but at no point in the film is there ever a parallel world and at no point is there even a suggestion that the two worlds exist simultaneously. Bottom line, there is no science in *Sliding Doors*. The story doesn't rely on science to be told, nor does science feature anywhere in it.

I hear similar arguments around films like *Groundhog Day* and *Big*, but both of those films are absolutely fantasy films. In *Groundhog Day*, a man gets stuck in a time loop and has to relive the same day over and over until he becomes a better man. The reason for this is kind of suggested as maybe having something to do with a mysterious snow storm — definitely not science — and the time loop ends when he finally reaches his goal of winning the heart of the woman he's fallen in love with. It's lovely and it's hysterically funny, but it's not science fiction. In *Big*, a boy grows to adult size after making a wish at a carnival machine. His way back to being kid-sized again is to track down the machine and make another wish. Again, not science fiction.

There are scores of films like this that get confused as being science fiction, when in fact they are fantasies, and it's easy to see how the lines between the two can be blurred. When it comes to writing, make sure you know in what genre your story falls. If it absolutely requires the science to drive the story forward, then it's a science fiction story and you need to be conscious of the science at all times while writing and make sure it's consistent and credible within its own world. If there is no science and the denouement relies on serendipity, or magic, or something intangible like love or kindness, then it's very likely you're writing a fantasy and that has its own set of rules to abide by.

WHY WRITE SCIENCE FICTION?

Why should I write science fiction? Honestly, I can't answer this one for you any more than I can answer the bigger question: *Why should I write?* Most people who write will tell you that it's because of a burning desire to tell stories. They write because they cannot imagine not writing, and that need to tell stories doesn't necessarily link itself to a particular genre, it's just there. I'll say now, if you want to write, and certainly if you want to write well and be successful, then you probably ought to feel the same way.

So let's approach this in a slightly different way. *What does science fiction offer that other genres do not?* Now that I can help you with, along with *What is science fiction good for?* and *What kinds of stories best lend themselves to science fiction?* All great questions, so let's get started.

The genre of ideas
Science fiction is often labeled "the genre of ideas" and that description really does sum up what great science fiction is all about. Writing science fiction is about asking the big "What if..?" questions, the questions that allow us to play with the day-to-day realities of our own world by exploring new and different realities in worlds we can create. Ultimately, science fiction is about allegory.

By using science fiction we can examine big social and societal issues and ask difficult and searching questions about subjects that concern all of us, and we can do it without pointing directly at any individual or group, any particular religion or country, any specific corporation or government. Science fiction allows us to shine a spotlight on something, bring it to the attention of the world, and say "Look at this! Look what is happening! Look what they've done!" And this is especially true if that something is out of our control or something we cannot easily change. It's small wonder that communist Eastern Europe produced so many fine science fiction writers over the years; if you cannot easily point at an injustice or an inequality and say "This is wrong!", then you can at least write about something very similar in order to get people to start talking about it.

Consider the current zeitgeist. What is it that keeps people up at night? What events or changes are we all truly concerned about? Global warming? Environmental damage? The threat of terrorism? Erosion of our civil liberties? CCTV and the lack of privacy? Rampant corporatisation? The poverty gap? Genetically modified crops? Energy saving? More than any other genre, science fiction deals directly with change. It's easy to point to technological change such as in medicine or biosciences, robotics or nanotechnology, and say "That's science fiction." But there are other, as important, changes that science fiction brings to our attention. Societal changes in our laws and freedoms, cultural changes in language and its use in communication, political changes in government and economics that bring about huge power shifts; no other genre will pay as much attention to these changes — and the consequence of these changes — as does science fiction.

Poster for *District 9* (2009).

Science fiction flips us out of our own cosy existence and our mundane concerns and forces us to think about our society in a different way. Whether the foundation of the message is built upon time travel, pandemic disease, parallel worlds, or a galaxy far, far away, it shows us that the usual way of doing things might not be the only way they could be done, that there may be a better way. But — and it's a very important but — science fiction rarely gives us the answers or preaches any kind of solution, it just gets the conversation started. Solutions are up to all of us to work out.

In the end it comes down to this. If you want to write about the nature of humanity and its relationship to the world around it, you pretty much have to write science fiction.

But....

Let's not forget that science fiction is also the perfect doorway to adventure and escapism. Science fiction lets us travel to hostile alien planets in far-flung galaxies and do battle with giant insects, travel backwards and forwards in time, discover the cure to a world-killing disease, blow-up an asteroid before it crashes into Earth, or be the last man left alive. It's no surprise to me that the early history of filmmaking went so quickly from social scenes and observations of the natural world to *A Trip To The Moon* (1902) because it's within us all to want to escape, to explore, and to make our mark. And science fiction, as a genre, tends to bite us pretty hard, usually at a very young age. For those bitten with the bug, it stays with us all our lives and, dare I say it, science fiction helps us to retain a youthful enthusiasm for new things in all parts of our lives, helping us keep our dreams alive. Anything you can think of, everything you ever wanted to see, all the amazing things that live in your imagination can find form in science fiction, and at the same time be contemporary, and relevant, and demonstrate important changes that will enlighten cinemagoers in ways other films cannot. In some rare and very special cases, science fiction can change the direction and future of mankind, and that's worth reaching for.

A GENRE OR A SETTING?

Given everything we've just discussed about why we should write in the science fiction genre, it probably seems more than a little strange that we're now going to discuss whether or not science fiction is even a genre at all. But the question isn't really, or at least not purely, one of writing. It's also an important question you need to ask yourself so that a) you can pitch your story properly, and b) someone from sales and/ or marketing can sell it.

The problem with science fiction is that, unlike other genres, it comes in all shapes and sizes. Romantic comedies are, well, romantic and funny, horror films are horrifying, dramas are dramatic, and thrillers are thrilling. But science fiction can be all of those things and be science-fictional. For example:

- *Star Man* — is a romance and a science fiction film.
- *Alien* — is a horror movie and a science fiction film.

- *E.T.: The Extra-Terrestrial* — is a family movie and a science fiction film.
- *The Terminator* — is an action movie and a science fiction film.
- *Never Let Me Go* — is a drama and a science fiction film.
- *Logan's Run* — is a thriller and a science fiction film.
- *Sleeper* — is a comedy and a science fiction film.

You can see the dilemma straight away. What exactly are you writing? Are you writing a Western set in space (*Outland*), or a *noir* detective story set in the far future (*Blade Runner*)? Is it a slasher movie pitting an alien against special forces soldiers (*Predator*), or is it a satirical thriller about a town populated by perfect housewives (*The Stepford Wives*)? As you might suspect, the genre lines are easily blurred.

All genres have their particular story beats. A romantic comedy has to have the "meet cute," action movies have their "Hamlet moment," thrillers generally have a compressed timeframe, and those things must be observed. When figuring out your story you will save yourself a whole lot of grief and aggravation if you figure out the primary genre and then write to the beats of that genre to start with. If you're writing a science fiction revenge chiller, then I would suggest that you actually plot a decent revenge chiller first and then as you re-write — and assuming the science is crucial to the story — build up the science fiction elements slowly, revealing your world through action and character rather than trying to build a sci-fi world and shoehorning a revenge chiller plot into it. You'll be rewarded with a far better screenplay if you do it that way, believe me.

There are, however some tropes that are pure science fiction because they just don't really fit anywhere else. And because of that they crop up in science fiction time and time again. That doesn't make them bad, just over-used, so if you find any of these in your story then you know a) you're writing a sci-fi, and b) you need to think differently about how you use them.

• Time Travel

No matter what kind of film you're writing, as soon as you add time travel to the mix it becomes a science fiction film. It can be as silly or incidental as you like, but time travel doesn't fit into any other genre. There are codas to this, of course. The time travel has to be deliberate and it has to be there to accomplish something. The character must go backward or forward in time in order to affect some kind of change and then return, or they accidentally travel through time and have to return to their own time without affecting anything. Someone just stuck in a *Groundhog Day*-type loop is not time-travelling — it's a fantasy concept, not science fiction.

• **Space Travel**
I don't include in this anything to do with the Apollo missions, the Space Shuttle, or anything else NASA has done in its glorious history, but rather any time you add easy, ubiquitous space travel (as in *Star Trek*) into your story. It really only fits into the science fiction bracket — or we'd all be doing it.

• **Post-Apocalyptic Worlds**
Another sci-fi-only element, because none of us have ever had to live in any kind of post-apocalyptic world, and therefore it must be speculative writing. It's also very common for settings like this to be the result of a catastrophic accident involving an advanced technology and the wanton hubris of man.

• **Alternate Histories**
If your story involves a different world to the one we know, then by and large it falls under the category of science fiction. It could be because of a historical event where the result turned out different-ly, such as in *C.S.A. The Confederate States of America* or *Death of a President*, or because it features a famous person who turns out to be totally different than the person we know from our history books, such as in *Abraham Lincoln: Vampire Hunter* (although it could easily be argued that the presence of vampires makes this a fantasy story).

• **Alien Beings/Worlds, Robots**
Not necessarily in a scary *Pitch Black* way or a cute *E.T.: The Extra-Terrestrial* way. *K-Pax* and *The Day the Earth Stood Still* have aliens at the core of the story. They mostly just talk and look like you and me, but their presence in the story makes these science fiction films. I'll also include robots here as another example of an alien being because,

despite the fact that they are made by humans, they have none of our humanity and are used in the same way as aliens, to hold a mirror up to ourselves.

● **Superpowers/Transformation/Mutation**
Anytime your main character develops a superpower like great strength, invisibility, incredible speed, or invulnerability, or if they start shrinking or growing at an alarming rate, or they suddenly stop ageing or turn into a fly, then you're writing science fiction.

So if it's all been done before, how do I transcend the genre?
This is probably the most difficult question of all and there really isn't a straightforward answer. The vast panoply of science fictional elements to choose from, and the ease with which they can be mixed and matched with any of the other story types, is one of the things that makes science fiction, to me, the most creatively open of all the genres. But truly memorable science fiction presents us with a new vision of how the world works and of how it can change and grow. If you can hold a mirror up to our world while building your own and show us how we might change, individually and collectively, to be better people and do things in a better way, then just maybe you will have created something truly special.

THE SCIENCE FICTION LANDSCAPE

The science fiction landscape is probably as broad as it gets in terms of the number and variety of sub-genres that fall underneath the larger heading. But whether you're writing **HARD SF**, where the sciences such as physics, chemistry, and biology, their various branches and related specialisms, are meticulously researched and 100% accurate, or **SOFT SF**, which centres around the social sciences, psychology, politics and government, communications, economics, law and so on, or even if you're from the making-it-up-as-you-go-along school, it's as well to know a number of these different flavours of science fiction and what characterises them, if only to make pitching your work easier. Some of these labels are well established as sub-genres within the science fiction community, others I've made-up or lumped together for the sake of brevity, but hopefully you'll recognise the "type" as soon as you read them.

9

Alternate history and alternate reality

Describes stories that take place in a world that has diverged significantly from the one we know, usually because the outcome of some major historical event was completely different to that in our history. Alternate histories are all about exploring the SOFT SF elements. In particular you'll find exploration of moral, ethical and/or social ideals, and these often go hand in hand with ideas about political or governmental change or very different thinking around religion. While an alternate history or alternate reality can be the basis for a story by itself, it can also quite often be part of a more pure science fictional story, such as entering a parallel universe.

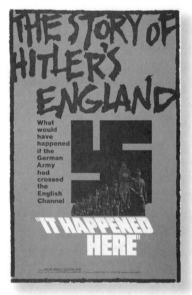

Poster for *It Happened Here* (1966).

As a sub-genre it's often combined with one of the "aesthetics" allowing the writer to draw upon an even larger store of ideas. **Steampunk**, for instance, lends itself well to alternate history in worlds where advanced technology — albeit steam-driven — has allowed man to explore further and conquer more than was actually possible and, as an aside, it's fair to say that Steampunk fans are a huge and at the moment very under-served part of the science fiction community. The **Cyberpunk** aesthetic, which was big in the 1980s, is equally well combined with alternate history, but more likely to be found as part of a dystopian world or a within a post-apocalyptic setting.

Good examples of alternate history are *Fatherland, C.S.A.: Confederate States of America, It Happened Here,* and *Timequest,* while some good examples of alternate realities are *Watchmen, White Man's Burden,* and *Southland Tales.*

A quick word about the "aesthetics"

A popular way of building an instant science fictional world is to choose one of the "aesthetics" and build on top of it. There are a number of these aesthetics. Some are very future-facing, extrapolated out of an always connected world, and others hark back to simpler times where the technology, while not as advanced, is still a great leap forward from what you'd expect. Within the science fiction community they are well known and can be leaned on to create instant shorthand for both writer and reader. Choosing a Cyberpunk aesthetic, for example, is an easy short-cut that says:

1) This is a science fiction story.
2) This is the kind of world it's in.
3) This is the kind of story you can expect.

Obviously this can work both ways. For the lazy writer it means they can just pluck a few Cyberpunk tropes out of the air and presto! They've turned their tired old thriller into a tired old science fiction thriller. But for the good writer — and that's you isn't it? I mean that's why you bought this book isn't it, to write better science fiction? — for you it's nothing more than a basis upon which to build your own world, a neat starting point that you can deconstruct and then re-construct with your own unique additional touches that will make it your own. As I said previously, there are a bunch of these, but the two most popular are:

"Cyberpunk" is a catch-all term for stories that take place in a future world of hugely advanced technology, ubiquitously wirelessly connected to an all-pervasive network of sophisticated artificial intelligences and biotechnology. Cyberpunk stories tend to be dystopian in nature, examining the effects on society, even on humanity itself, of unchecked perpetual technological advance and ubiquitous data-flow. In Cyberpunk futures the world is often run by a single giant corporation in league with a corrupt government, with both of them prepared to offer any sacrificial lamb upon the altar of financial profit. The inhabitants of these futures usually fall into two categories: the rich "Haves" and the poor "Have-nots," with the story revolving around a single hero or a group of people fighting the system to even things up.

Keanu Reeves plugs in. (*Johnny Mnemonic*, 1995)

Blade Runner, *Johnny Mnemonic*, *Strange Days*, and *New Rose Hotel* are all good examples of a Cyberpunk aesthetic.

"Steampunk" tales are set generally in the Victorian era (or something very similar). The central idea in Steampunk is that the industrial revolution heralded much more innovation than we currently imagine and steam technology became far more advanced than the real technology of the time ever did. Thus, in combination with clockwork or mechanical engines, steam is used to power everything from trains and carriages to tanks, dirigibles, assorted weaponry, and even robots. Alongside this is a very Victorian aesthetic in design and manufacturing, with complex gadgets being fashioned from brass and leather and featuring delicate balances, glowing valves and intricately wrought engraving. Steampunk is often mashed up with various science fiction and fantasy tropes that allow the writer to employ recognisably modern gadgetry in a gas-powered or clockwork form. Thus characters can do something as simple as carry a communication device (rather than a mobile phone) or as complex as ride in a giant bipedal mechanoid (instead of a humble tank). Of course the fashion, manners and social and class structures of Victorian times also colour Steampunk storytelling, making for a

There's nothing more "Steampunk" than airships. (*The Three Musketeers*, 2011)

distinct style of dialogue, but so does a very Victorian attitude to exploration and adventure which lends itself perfectly to storytelling

Check out *The Three Musketeers, Sherlock Holmes, The Golden
Compass, Steamboy, The League of Extraordinary Gentlemen, Wild
Wild West*, and TV's *Warehouse 13*. (Much of the technology in this
fun TV series has a Steampunk aesthetic, reflecting some of the origins
of the Warehouse itself.)

Alien Encounters
Encounters with alien beings assume various guises in science fiction, but
do broadly fall into three categories.

First Contact stories mostly explore the initial communications between
humans and aliens. This can be as simple as a radio signal (*Contact*) or as
threatening as a flying saucer landing in Presidents Park South (*The Day
The Earth Stood Still*) but the core idea of these stories is usually the same;
either by observing the aliens or by watching ourselves through their eyes
we are really holding a mirror up to ourselves and asking "What does
it mean to be human?" Once again we are exploring the SOFT SF elements, and often in this case we are asking about religion and about belief. What does it do to those things once we know there is alien life out
there and it is more technologically advanced than we are?

The other little-utilised flavours of First Contact are the comedy and the romance, but they do exist and have had some success with audiences. They too use the situation to hold a mirror up to ourselves for examination, and the questions they ask can be as searching as in any other sub-genre, but the approach to them does tend to have a lighter touch. In the case of comedy it is saying "Look at us! Look at how silly we are! Look at how we behave towards each other and see how inconsequential the things we hold dear really are." Examples of science fiction comedy would be *My Favorite Martian, Brother From Another Planet, Coneheads,* and *Paul.* With romance we are digging a little deeper with questions about what love means, what companionship means, about whether we lose the ability to empathise without love or without a partner, and of course can we love someone who is completely alien to ourselves. Snuggle up on the sofa with *Kate & Leopold* or *Star Man* for examples of romantic science fiction.

Jenny Hayden (Karen Allen) falls in love with Starman (Jeff Bridges). (*Starman,* 1984)

The natural extension from First Contact is the **Alien Invasion** story in which an immense invasion force comprising huge spacecraft with incredible firepower and complete invulnerability ravage the

Earth, destroying everything in their path — especially us, those pesky Earthlings — for no good reason often enough, or else in order to "consume our natural resources" or some such foolishness. Obvious examples are *Independence Day*, *The War of the Worlds*, *Invasion of the Body Snatchers*, *The Day of the Triffids*, and the TV show *Falling Skies*. These are by far the most popular alien encounter stories, which is a shame because it says much about us that we view all "alien encounters" as an attack, a potential threat to be annihilated by any means possible. Now don't get me wrong — I'll sit back with a giant popcorn and supersize soda and watch the big guns and the explosions, I'll cheer at the inevitable fight back where we, as a species, come together and kick alien butt, and I'll have as much fun and enjoy it as much as the next guy. But it's a bit like that popcorn and soda — okay to fill you up for a couple of hours but not substantial enough to stop the hunger. In a "genre of ideas," we need better ones than this.

The final category in the alien encounters stream is the **Monster Movie**, and there's a ton of 'em. In general they take the form of the horror-movie "stalk 'n' slash" film where a creature or creatures unknown stalk, attack, and kill a group of people one by one until finally the last one left figures out how to beat them. Alternatively, and this doesn't happen quite so often, the creature(s) can be big enough to make it into a city and terrorise the inhabitants, but the basic plot is the same, just on a much bigger scale. Monster Movies are by and large cautionary tales. Our species has brought this upon ourselves through scientific hubris or environmental catastrophe, or by wanton colonisation of lands we shouldn't have annexed. Monster Movies also allow audiences to be frightened, which is a thrill most of us rarely experience outside of the darkness of the cinema. Occasionally, when the monster in question has a human element or is particularly malevolent, then monster movies show us inside the darkest heart of our own human behaviour. Monster Movies speak to our great fear of the unknown and have adapted through the ages to explore the threat of atomic power, the rise of communism, the dumping of toxic waste, depletion of the Earth's resources, and the unchecked experimentation with biotechnology. The monster that stalks us embodies all these things — and if we don't learn from our mistakes, it will kill us in the end.

There are a few tropes for this kind of movie. Be aware of them and then, as usual, subvert and transcend them as you will to raise your Monster Movie above the crowd. Trope number one involves the group doing something they shouldn't have, or not doing something they should have, the consequence of which unleashes the monster so the fun can begin. Trope number two is that the creature is only acting according to instinct, it's not hunting people out of malice and often it's only doing it to protect territory upon which the humans have somehow trespassed, so we can, if not sympathise, then empathise with it. The character tropes are the same as for most horror films of this kind: the poorly fleshed-out character that will die early, the love interest who the hero will need to rescue, and the mentor who warns everyone of the folly of their behaviour very early on.

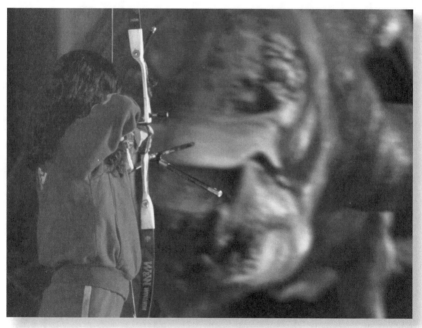

You never know what's lurking in the sewers. (*The Host,* 2006)

Take your pick from *Splice, Jurassic Park, The Host, Cloverfield, Pitch Black,* or *Alien.*

Apocalyptic Events and Post-Apocalyptic Futures

Apocalyptic Events — more commonly known as "disaster movies" — generally take place in the present day or in the very near future. These events are usually preceded by years of warnings that man has ignored, and now that things have begun to fall apart it's far too late to do anything about it. There is often the suggestion that this is nature's way of spring-cleaning the Earth, like it's a giant, cosmic reset button, although our species will survive. So what audiences want to know is "Who will survive and how will they do it?" It's also a chance to see giant asteroids blow up Paris or massive tidal waves engulf New York, because we all know that great spectacle is a big part of apocalyptic events. Typical movies include *The Day After Tomorrow*, *Armageddon*, *The Core*, *Knowing*, *Volcano*, *Deep Impact*, and *When Worlds Collide*.

Post-Apocalyptic Futures are the natural extension of apocalyptic events as they are set in the aftermath of the global extinction. They tend to examine how humans behave towards each other during the worst of times, and often, the answer is "Not well." Food, water, and basic necessities are usually scarce and the driving force of the stories is survival, but the world will almost always divide into the "Haves" and "Have-nots" and the focus of conflict will often be along these lines.

Max (Mel Gibson) hits the road with his best friend. *(Mad Max 2: The Road Warrior, 1981)*

Films in this category come in many shapes and sizes, but can include variations on nuclear warfare, global pandemic, natural disaster (tsunami, earthquake, ice-age), impact events (giant asteroid), rise of the machines (robots and computers kill us all), dysgenics (genetic disorders such as female inability to conceive), and climate change, and the results give us variations on last-man-alive, survival-of-the-fittest, the wild west, and everyone's favourite — zombies!

Check out *Doomsday, The Road, The Postman, Waterworld, Ever Since The World Ended, Mad Max 2: The Road Warrior, The Book of Eli, I Am Legend, The Hunger Games*, and *28 Days Later*.

Dystopian/Utopian Futures
While they may seem different on the surface, these two are basically the same film with one vital exception. The **Dystopian Future** is unremittingly grim from the opening scene. There are problems with the atmosphere or with basic resources, food shortages, and a lack of medical care are regular elements of the dystopia and the world is run by a ruling authority that exercises total control of the inhabitants, often with extremely harsh punishments meted out to anyone who transgresses the law. This world is not one that we would want to live in. **Utopian Futures**, on the other hand, seem idyllic on the surface, everyone seems happy and content and in good health with a surplus of leisure time, but beneath this perfect facade things are often just as grim as in the dystopian world, with an extremely poor underclass battling to survive under desperate circumstances.

The recurring themes of both of these types of story are loss of freedom and loss of control over one's own life. The ultimate extrapolation of the "Nanny State," where individual freedoms have been ceded to the state in order that the state can decide what is best for you and for everyone around you. Other science fictional elements that crop up are the dying Earth, somehow unable to support human life for much longer due to man-made catastrophe; rampant globalisation crushing cultural and social differences, throwing them into a meat grinder and pushing out a homogenised one-size-fits-all global community at the other end; and the rise of the corporation to a position of ultimate power, willing to do whatever it takes to retain power and grow profits.

It's not unusual to think of these stories taking place in the period of time between the apocalyptic event and the post-apocalyptic world.

Sam Lowry (Jonathan Pryce) chats with the local kids. *(Brazil, 1985)*

There are a great many of these kinds of films to choose from, but you won't go far wrong with *Children of Men, Brazil, Code 46, Gattaca, Equilibrium, The Handmaid's Tale, 1984, Farenheit 451,* or *Logan's Run.*

Space Opera/Space Western

Sitting firmly in the HARD SF camp, **Space Operas** and **Space Westerns** are at the same time the worst of science fiction and the best of science fiction. More often than not, exactly like an old-fashioned western of the kind you haven't seen in a multiplex in many a long year, they are stories of the brave and bold, explorers opening up new frontiers, clearing the way for ordinary folk to follow on and build towns and start farms and begin mining and trading and all the other stuff that frontier towns have to do. Of course that means that there will be "good guys" keeping everyone straight and maintaining the law, and "bad guys" in the shape of other people or alien beings or carnivorous plants or armies of killer robots or whatever it might be and they will need to be overcome for the greater good of mankind, and all of this can happen in the farthest reaches of space or on a single newly colonised planet.

These can be fantastic stories of adventure and derring-do, giving us unique insight into the social and technological problems man
would face if he reached out to the stars in earnest. They can explore
interstellar travel and faster-than-light theories, touch on new types of
politics and religion, diplomacy, trade with alien species, problems of
language and communication, health and wellbeing and so much more,
and they can be amongst the greatest science fiction stories of them all.
Unfortunately, they can also be hackneyed old tales of white hats and
black hats, riddled with cliché and stiff with scientific implausibilities
and vague technical explanations. These latter examples are why your
contemporaries sneered at you at school and why your parents frowned
at your growing collection of genre books. Please, write the good stuff
and move the genre forward. It can still be exciting and fun and adventurous — just make it good as well.

I'm going to slot into this mix the stalwart **Military Science Fiction**,
which is very much the same kind of idea as the Space Western, except
that the story centres around combat in space or on distant planets
against the same selection of bad guy humans, aliens, plants, robots and
so on. The key difference here being a huge array of high-tech weaponry, and in some cases, the combatants themselves being genetically
modified for the sole purpose of fighting in these new conditions. The
obvious themes here are anti-war, as you would expect, but, like all war

There's trouble brewing for Johnny Rico (Casper Van Dien). *(Starship Troopers, 1997)*

films, there is often a side theme of brothers-in-arms, of camaraderie unique to men who go to war with each other, and of ordinary people showing extraordinary courage in the face of overwhelming odds. These are the guys who fight so that the rest of us don't have to, and it would be good to remember that from time to time.

Spend some time with *Starship Troopers*, *Serenity*, *Battlestar Galactica* (TV), *Space Battleship Yamato*, *Space: Above and Beyond* (TV), *Farscape* (TV), *Babylon 5* (TV), *John Carter*.

Superhero/Superpowers

Everyone knows the superhero archetype, someone who has a super ability or special power and uses that power in a heroic manner, to do good, fight crime, and ensure justice prevails. Almost without exception they spring from the pages of comic books or graphic novels and they are so numerous that they provide rich pickings for filmmakers beyond just the obvious commercial potential of a readymade fanbase. Good superheroes are rich and complex characters, the best ones being far from perfect, and their background often includes some kind of traumatic experience which goes a long way towards defining who they are, because rather than collapse under the weight of that trauma, they exhibit a mental strength that allows them to overcome the trauma and make meaning of their lives.

Like all good science fiction, these stories also explore our society and the advances in technology and science that seem to be de-humanising us to the extent that we have forgotten how to behave towards each other. While the big crime boss or supervillain is a key ingredient to a lot of superhero stories, very often the bad guys our hero has to face come in the form of a corrupt politician, a greedy corporation, a totalitarian regime, or a warring government, and in fighting and defeating them our superhero is showing us a better way to behave. It's important to point out that the use of a mask and cape is optional, but it does give the ordinary-life character something to hide behind while fighting for good. Anyone who has ever dressed up in a costume will describe the feeling of being a different person, somehow better, more open, more interested and interesting and much more empowered. A costume is a good way of hiding your old identity, but it's also the perfect way of bringing out the new. In rare cases they can look good, too.

We know that a superhero will fight for justice and sacrifice himself for others, and these selfless values and heroic actions are there to inspire others to more pro-social behaviour. That doesn't mean we should fly or leap tall buildings or fight bad guys, but, just as our favourite superheroes have different powers and abilities, we each have something we can use, like time or money, or something we can sacrifice, like energy or commitment, to help others in our own way.

Superheroes have an enduring appeal because often they are outsiders. They are weak, or they are bullied, or they feel misunderstood. They have an ability that makes them different and, often at a time when they just want to blend in and be accepted, they are forced to face the responsibility of who they are and what they can achieve. Sounds a bit like being told by your parents that you need to grow up and make something of yourself, doesn't it? But superheroes are also compelling because while they seem just like us — albeit an upgraded version of us — we also wonder how we would behave if we had their power and we all like to think we would stand up and be the hero in our story.

There are so many superhero films to pick from: *The Green Lantern, Superman, Spider Man, Iron Man, X-Men, Hellboy,* and *Daredevil* for starters.

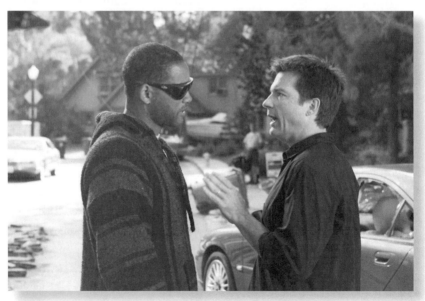

Ray (Jason Bateman) teaches Hancock (Will Smith) the subtle art of diplomacy. (*Hancock,* 2008)

Recently there has been a trend towards exploring the darker side of having a superpower, where the recipient of the power turns out not to be a good person, or at least not squeaky clean, and they decide to use their power for some kind of personal gain, but the results, predictably, see the wrongdoer hoisted on their own petard. We don't get this kind of subversion of the superhero too often, but I believe we will see more of these types of stories over the coming years. I think we'll especially see elements of these stories mashed-up with romance, comedy, and horror.

Examples: *X-Men*, *My Super Ex-Girlfriend*, *Hancock*, *Scott Pilgrim vs. The World*, *Chronicle*.

Mundane Science Fiction

Mundane Science Fiction deals with real science and real technology on this Earth. Mundane SF posits that "ordinary" science fiction is too reliant on running away from our own world rather than taking a look at the world around us, and thus sets out to do just that, setting stories in the very near future, either on or very close to Earth, featuring science and technology as it exists at the time the story is written and being utilised in a believable way.

The key elements of Mundane Science Fiction are no interstellar travel (and therefore no earth-like worlds for us to colonise), no evidence of intelligent life elsewhere in the universe (and therefore no interstellar trade or communication), and the outlook that our most likely future is on this planet and within this solar system, with only ourselves for company.

Despite the perceived limitations of the "Mundane Manifesto," it is possible to write stories about a huge number of near future topics that will affect us all, for example the destruction of the planet's resources through over consumption, massive climate change, and pollution provide fertile soil for mundane stories, as does the unknown effects of advances in biotechnology, but there are other societal issues to look at like the effects of constant CCTV surveillance on public behaviour and police work and how far it will go, how the Internet is changing politics and will continue to change politics forever, and how globalisation is eroding and homogenising our cultural individualities.

Mundane Science Fiction stories illustrate how these kinds of societal changes and technological advances might change us, and explore the issues that we might encounter as humans. But at their heart, like all good stories, they are about people, about families, and about how they are altered by the world around them, and across the science fiction landscape this is the biggest area for growth in films and screenplays.

While there aren't any films specifically marketed as "Mundane" (and you can see why, who would go and see a "mundane" film?) a number of those I've already mentioned deal with possible real-world issues that fall under the "mundane" remit. They include *Code 46* (genetics, immigration, and population control), *Gattaca* (genetics, eugenics) *Children of Men* (pandemic, fertility, societal breakdown), *Ever Since The World Ended* (post-pandemic society), *2033* (freedom, state controls, totalitarian government), and *The Age of Stupid* (climate change).

EXERCISE ONE

So I'm going to take a giant leap-in-the-dark here and assume that you've got an idea for a film and you think it might make a good science fiction movie.

Based on what we've learned so far, ask yourself a couple of questions:

1) What KIND of science fiction movie is it? Is it action? Drama? Romance? Remember, science fiction can be as much a setting that enhances your story as it is a genre, and it's as well you figure out the primary drivers for your narrative BEFORE you start writing. Is it actually a thriller or a comedy or some other genre with just a science fiction veneer?

2) Having taken the time to decide what kind of science fiction film it is, you should now examine your story idea. Look at it objectively and ask yourself: Is this really a science fiction film? Consider the following:

- Are your science fiction elements real or are you just using one of the aesthetics?

- Does your story rely on the science in order to be told?
- Is the science in your story deliberate and purposeful?
- Is your story about the science or is it about the effects of the science on the characters?
- If your story is definitely science fiction, into which sub-genre of the landscape does it fit?

After all that, if you're positive that you have a science fiction story on your hands, then brilliant! Skip the next chapter and go straight to chapter three, Creating Characters. If you decide that actually it's not really a science fiction film, then that's also good — at least you've found out now — and if you're still up for writing science fiction, then the next chapter, Finding Your Story, is going to be perfect for you.

Extra Credit
Once you've answered satisfactorily that your story is science fiction, ask yourself why you're writing in this genre? What does it offer that other genres don't? Do you need to use allegory to tell your story, or is there another reason? If you just want to write a futuristic thriller, then that's great, I *love* futuristic thrillers. But in order for it to really work, you need to have some sense of the big, over-arching "What if..?" question you're trying to explore. Knowing this will deepen your story and make it much more likely to connect with readers and audiences.

CHAPTER TWO

FINDING YOUR STORY

FINDING THE FUTURE IN THE PRESENT

It's not how you come up with the idea that really counts, it's how you move forward with the idea and turn it into a screenplay that will distinguish you.

The lazy man's way of coming up with science fiction film ideas has traditionally been to take any movie title you can think of and add "in space!" to the end of it. Like *High Noon*... in space! (*Outland*), *Jaws*... in space! (*Alien*), *The Swiss Family Robinson*... in space! (*Lost in Space*), and so on. There's some validity in this, and over the years it's become a tried and trusted method of idea generation, but while it has led to the occasional classic — no one is going to argue against *Alien* being a sci-fi classic — there are a lot more films in the mediocre pile.

So where do we find the ideas ripe for science fiction treatment?

Well, as you might expect, they're all around you. In the news, on the web, in magazines and journals, and in your local library. They come from TV programs, documentaries, and other movies you might watch. All you have to do is start looking, and pretty soon you'll realise it's not finding an idea that's the problem, it's choosing from the hundreds of ideas that will present themselves to you.

Remember, though, that science fiction dates at a much faster pace than other genres. If you look at the wonderfully futuristic spaceships of the 1950s, they look like early NASA designs, and I remember watching an old episode of *Thunderbirds* with my son where Scott Tracy received an image over the "tele-image transponder" or some such — basically a fax machine — which seemed quaint to me back then, but in these days of email and camera phones feels positively ancient!

When you're picking your stories, don't fixate on the science or the technology, you're looking for the human story behind that. You're looking for the effect that the science or technology has on people, on how they think, how they react, how they treat each other. It's not the science and technology that's important, it's the ramifications of the science and technology.

EVERDAY TOOLS FOR COLLECTING IDEAS

I collect ideas for science fiction stories every day. Some days it'll be just one, some days I'll find a half dozen, sometimes I won't get the basis of a full story but I'll find an interesting element that can serve as a plot point for another bigger story. The only days I don't find an idea are the days I'm not looking, and even then they still occasionally jump into my lap.

I don't usually name names, but my search for ideas involves the following:
1) An Internet connection.
2) An RSS newsreader or Newsreader account (I use a Mac, my reader is called Vienna and it's free).
3) A web browser.
4) A web-clipping account (I use Evernote, which is also free).

Those are the basic tools of the trade, but in addition I do have:
1) Text editing software.
2) An "Ideas" folder on my hard drive.
3) A notepad and pen.
4) A dictation/voice recorder app on my mobile phone.

Okay, this is how I got started.

Write down a list of the kind of news that you think would be useful. To get you started, try searching for things like medical technology, futurists, space news, gadgets, architecture, agriculture, social trends, and business strategy and entrepreneurialism.

Assuming you're connected to the Internet, download and install your RSS Newsreader on your computer.

Next, start surfing the web for your chosen topics. When you find a website that's full of interesting stories, look for the symbol shown here.

This is the symbol for RSS (Really Simple Syndication) that indicates that there is a regularly updated feed

RSS Feed icon.

of news items from that site. Open your reader and subscribe to the feed from that site — a process that varies from machine to machine and reader to reader. Do this with all the interesting sites that you find. This will take time, you won't find all the interesting stuff in one day, and it helps to organise your feeds into folders so that you can find them easily if necessary.

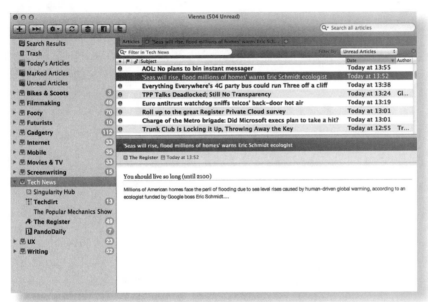

My RSS Reader. You can see the folders, an indicator telling me how many unread items in each, and a story I've highlighted that will definitely bear closer inspection.

Spend some time every day perusing all the news feeds in your RSS reader. When you come across a headline that looks interesting, click on it and open up the full story in your web browser. Having set up a web clipping account, if the story looks promising or you think it's interesting in some way, clip it and save it into your account so that you can study it later. Remember to tag it properly and give it an understandable title so that you can find it when you search for it.

My web clipping account. You can see the folder structure I'm using and a few of the stories I have clipped.

If you don't have an Internet connection, then go to your local library and use theirs. You can set up free accounts online that will allow to gather news feeds and clip stories for later and it works just as well with the exception that you can't take it with you — but that's why you have a notepad and pen.

When you've collected a few stories and a few interesting snippets, it's time to play the "What if..?" game.

"WHAT IF..?" AND THE VAST POOL OF STORY SOURCES

As we discussed in the first chapter, good science fiction is concerned with the state of things now. It extrapolates on current thinking and current concerns and asks the big "What if..?" questions. Let's play a little "What if..?" right now.

Using my RSS Newsreader I came across this story at DailyGalaxy. com a few months ago and thought it was a tremendous source for a story idea.

According to the piece, plans are being drawn up for a "Dooms-day Ark" to be built on the moon by the European Space Agency. The Ark will contain the essentials of life and human civilisation and will be activated in the event that Earth is devastated by a giant asteroid or nuclear war. This lunar information bank would provide survivors on Earth with a remote-access toolkit to rebuild the human race.

Ark 1.0 would contain hard discs holding information such as DNA sequences and useful instructions such as how to smelt metal or information about agriculture. It would be sealed in a vault and buried just below the Moon's surface, with transmitters sending the data to heavily protected receivers on earth. If no receivers survive, the Ark will continue transmitting the information until new receivers can be built. Ark 2.0 would later be extended to include a diversity of species from the biosphere, natural material such as microbes, animal embryos, and plant seeds and even cultural relics such as surplus items from museum stores. Presumably version 2.0 will also have a social networking element.

So let's play "What if..?"

What if we had advance warning of Earth being destroyed by an asteroid? We can't call Bruce Willis, but we do have sufficient time to deploy a doomsday ark and maybe some people with it. What would it need to contain? What's important? What isn't? How do you judge and who makes that call? This isn't just about what "stuff" we should take, this is about what is the essence of humanity, and frankly, is it worth saving?

What if the only people selected to save were scientists and politicians? What if they held a lottery? What if it turned out they were all white? Would they try to change things around or go with the best-qualified people? What would be the criteria?

Equally important is what we would leave out.

What if we didn't include information about religion or politics? A new humanity will have enough to worry about without elections and worship, but concepts like government and church can impose order on chaos and help folk make sense of their lives. This is deep, rich stuff for a film to tackle.

WRITING THE SCIENCE FICTION FILM ROBERT GRANT

Now lets go the other way.

What if the information was wrong or got corrupted in some way and we re-start the human race totally differently to what was originally envisaged? What could go wrong? Were the genetic codes wrong? Did the seeds and embryos we sent up become horribly mutated? Are we leaving a destroyed Earth just to end up destroying the Moon? Is it in our natures to just destroy everything wherever we decide to lay our hats? That's an interesting theme to work through.

You can see how a simple news item can be the basis of a lot of "What if..?" questions and can lead to ideas for a very interesting science fiction film. But while this film is a more thoughtful film than most, we can always switch it up for a different feel.

What if the survivors split into factions and refused to co-operate? *What if* someone was murdered and crop seeds were stolen? Could a black market in rare food crops precipitate a thriller?

There's a lot of different ways to go here, depending on whether our story starts before, during, or after the Ark is launched, but the exercise is the same. Spend time thinking "What if..?" and you'll be amazed at how many ideas are generated, and the more you dig into an idea, the more rewards you'll find. Of course none of this by itself will give you a completed story, but enough of these ideas together will give you a great foundation upon which to build one.

CLOSE TO HOME OR FAR, FAR AWAY?

A key part of playing the "What if..?" game while you're trying to find your story is *when* your story is going to take place. To a certain extent this is going to be dictated by any initial ideas you might have had, but beyond that the choices are fairly straightforward; do you want to set your story in the present day, a few years into the future, or many hundreds or even thousands of years from now? It may not seem so important right now, but whatever choice you make is going to have a big impact on the world you build, and often, a lot of what can or cannot happen in your story.

Setting your story in the present day has many advantages; your audience knows the world of the story, they understand the culture, religion, media, science and technology, and that gives you an instant shorthand. It also allows you to tap into the zeitgeist; what are people worried about, what are the current concerns the general populace has about government, education, medicine, science, technology and faith. These are things you can easily tap for story ideas. Everywhere you turn there are scary stories about the power of the media, global epidemics, erosion of our freedoms, obesity, the war machine, climate change, food additives and poverty. These are rich veins for science fiction to tap, but if you add to them the possibility of alien invasion or the coming zombie apocalypse, you can see why setting a science fiction film in the present day has such appeal. No one wants to see their world turned upside down, but we all worry that it might happen and we also think that we'll be the ones to survive.

Near Future — say fifty to a hundred years away — is probably the hardest place to set any story but can also be the most rewarding. As I write this, the year 2050 is thirty-eight years away. This may not seem like much in science fiction terms, but if you think back thirty-eight years to 1974, it's clear that there have been massive changes in every conceivable part of our lives since then. Pointing out the technological advances is easy. You can laugh (and I know you will) but when I was a kid in the UK, not everyone had a colour TV and there were only three channels, two of which didn't start broadcasting till late afternoon. Now we have 500 channels of all-digital, surround-sound, hi-definition TV, 24 hours a day. Technologies have been invented and become obsolete in that time. We've gone from vinyl to the cassette tape to the MP3, from VHS to Blu-ray to MP4, from 35mm film to videotape to digital cameras. We're currently heading from printed books to eBooks and right now the advances in mobile phones and cloud technology pose a significant threat to sales of everything from landlines, to digital cameras and laptops, to wristwatches. But that's just the tip of the iceberg. When we look at changes to culture, religion, media, health and welfare, work, transport and travel, the law... really, the list is endless and the changes vast, and that's how you must think if you're looking at Near Future science fiction.

Far Future — well, you can really have anything here that you can dream up, as long as you can convince an audience of its likelihood or validity (and we'll get to that). Space travel, robots, sentient animal companions, alien worlds — these are the things we've come to expect from far future stories, but they don't have to be tales of adventure and derring-do. There's as much drama to be had in the lives of ordinary people and their day-to-day dramas as there is in travelling to extraordinary worlds and shooting everything you see.

It might help your thinking if we bastardise a quote from ex-U.S. Secretary of Defence Donald Rumsfeld for some elements to consider in your planning:

The known knowns — the things that we know are almost upon us in terms of new technology, medicine, media, communications, social and political change, cultural points of view, and so on. We can fairly confidently say that these things are coming. If you write present-day sci-fi you will likely go here a lot.

The known unknowns — these are the things that might come along, things that feel like they should be on their way but we currently either don't know enough about them, or lack the sufficient technology to develop them to say if they will definitely come to pass. That doesn't mean they won't, new breakthroughs happen all the time, but we don't know for certain. Near Future writers will visit here regularly.

The unknown unknowns — this is the stuff that we don't know about, couldn't possibly know about, and so we cannot predict any outcome. The real "out-there-like-Pluto" stuff that defines both genius and madman. You will go here occasionally, but, if you have any sense, you won't stay long.

Any one of these knowns or unknowns can influence your story as a positive or a negative, it's up to you how you use them. An *unknown unknown* could be that aliens land in Parliament Square but they bring with them a cure for cancer — a positive story. A *known known* would be the incumbent government deciding to keep this cure and wield it for political or financial gain, thus your story becomes a negative. It feels as if traditional Hollywood fare will always seek the negative because it provides easy conflict and, as we all know, conflict drives your story. But it doesn't have to be that way.

Exercise Two

༄

This is the abridged version of a news article I found at TheRegister.
co.uk early in 2012.

Stolen NASA Laptop had Space Station Control Codes
A NASA laptop stolen last year had not been encrypted, despite contain-
ing codes used to control and command the International Space Station,
the agency's inspector general told a U.S. House committee.

NASA IG Paul Martin said in written testimony to the House Committee
on Science, Space and Technology that a laptop was stolen in March
2011, which "resulted in the loss of the algorithms used to command
and control the ISS." As well as facing the continuous disappearance of
unencrypted staff laptops, NASA is also subject to increasingly sophis-
ticated cyber attacks, Martin told the hearing. "In 2010 and 2011,
NASA reported 5,408 computer security incidents from individuals,
well-organised criminal enterprises and foreign intelligence services seeking
to further their countries' objectives."

Scary stuff, huh? Well now's your chance. I want you to spend an
hour thinking about this news story and playing the "What if..?" game.
To make it easy, spend a couple of minutes on each of the questions
below and don't forget — this sounds like a thriller based in a contemporary USA, but it doesn't have to be.

- What is the worst thing that could happen?
- What is the best thing that could happen?
- Are they the same thing?
- Who is directly affected?
- Who is indirectly affected?
- Who stands to win from this?
- Who stands to lose from this?
- Who will get rich?
- How will they get rich?
- Who will lose out?
- How will they lose out?

Try and answer these questions, but as you do, extrapolate out to find in-depth answers, don't settle for one-word responses.

Then we'll take a look at characters.

CHAPTER THREE

CREATING CHARACTERS

BUT IT'S ABOUT PEOPLE, RIGHT?

Science fiction films have a reputation for being all about spectacle, a not entirely unfounded criticism when you look at a lot of what's out there. But at the heart of any good science fiction film, in common with good films of any genre, is a story about people. We may love the thrills and spills in *Inception*, but what we really want to know is will Cobb get back to his children? And in *Source Code*, while Colter Stevens is trying to find and stop the train bomber, what we really care about is will he end up with Christina Warren?

As an audience we don't change and grow alongside the characters we watch. But in the same way that our friends and family, colleagues and peers will have an influence on our appearance, our thinking, and our behaviour, so the people we watch in films and on TV — especially those we strongly identify with, those that resonate emotionally — will no doubt have an influence on us.

As a science fiction writer this presents you with an amazing opportunity. If you're writing good science fiction you are revealing something of this world through allegory. This is your chance to communicate an idea with a great many people, a chance to maybe change the world. But no one wants to be preached to. As movie producer Samuel Goldwyn famously said, "If you want to send a message, use Western Union." So you cannot get on your soapbox to get your idea across. You have a tell a story, and good stories are about people.

A note about dialogue

It's worth bearing in mind that good groundwork on your characters and their relationships to each other will help enormously when it comes to writing dialogue. Where someone comes from, events from their past, and how they are as a person will have a huge influence on their patterns of speech, their confidence, and indeed their willingness to talk, and how someone views someone else will influence what they say — whether they are supportive or condescending, interested or bored, trusting or untrusting, and so on. Spend a little time on this stuff now and it can save you a lot of time later on.

WHO IS YOUR HERO, AND WHY THAT GUY?

There's a reason why Del Spooner (Will Smith) is the main character in *I, Robot*. It's because in a film about a murder that may have been committed by a robot, the best person to investigate the crime is a robot-phobic detective. Even better when he is a good friend of the victim, better yet that he suffers survivors guilt over a car accident where a robot saved him rather than a 12-year-old girl, even more so because Spooner has a robotic arm as a result. As the story unfolds, Spooner has to grow and change in his resentment and suspicion of robots. Eventually, despite his suspicions proving to have some foundation, but at a much greater level than he could possibly imagine, he has to overcome his prejudice in order to defeat the bigger threat.

Del Spooner (Will Smith) just doesn't trust robots. (*I, Robot,* 2004)

When you see it laid out like this it's easy to see the who and why of that character, but it's true of all stories in all genres, not just science fiction, and you'd do well to remember it. *The main character in your story has to be the only person this story could possibly happen to.* They cannot be some random person off the street who just happened to stumble into the story. Even if the initial set-up of the story is written that way, eventually we should find out that your random stranger is actually the only person that this story could possibly have happened to.

You'll see these traits referred to as flaws or wounds in many books, but a single flaw or wound is not enough for your hero. There has to be several of them, each small in its way, but when they are layered one upon the other they make the perfect protagonist.

In *Stargate*, Dr. Daniel Jackson (James Spader) is not just an Egyptologist, he is an Egyptologist with an outlandish theory that the Great Pyramid at Giza was actually built by beings from outer space. That's almost enough right there, but in order to make him uniquely useful to the story — and to the military program — he's also an expert in linguistics, specifically ancient Egyptian languages, but even that's not enough. We have to make sure he has no choice but to go on this journey, so when we meet him he's reached his nadir, ridiculed by his peers with nowhere else to go and, as Dr. Catherine Langford (Viveca Lindfors) tells him "*...you've just been evicted out of your apartment, your grants have run out, everything you own is in those two bags. You wanna prove that your theories are right? This is your chance.*"

Dr. Daniel Jackson (James Spader) goes for broke. (*Stargate*, 1994)

So when you've found your story and played a little "What if..?", your hero, their characteristics, skills, experiences, and their place in the world should, to a large extent, become self-evident. Sure there's a lot more to it than that, but you can use the same logic in many ways. Are they male or female? Well, if your story world is male-dominated, it could be that a female protagonist going against the odds provides a better viewpoint. If they need to investigate something, then they need investigative skills, or at least that mindset, so for an occupation we can choose a cop, a private detective, a journalist, a scientist, someone whose day-to-day activities involve investigation or research.

If we dig a little bit deeper we can start to address their world view and their moral and ethical code of conduct that will colour how they speak and how they act towards others. Are they curt with people and bad tempered, or are they everyone's friend? Are they a loner who can't socialise, or are they the life and soul of every party? The more you do this, the more you think through these things, the more depth and three-dimensionality you will imbue your characters with. There are whole books devoted to creating characters but at their core your hero should always be the one and only person that this story could possibly happen to, the perfect person to become involved in these events.

<h2 style="text-align:center">SIDEKICKS AND BUDDIES</h2>

Buddies are there to help, support, and encourage the hero so that he can solve the great problem. Buddies are useful. They can each repre-sent a part of the hero's life or personality that is missing and they can fulfill roles that the hero cannot by being smarter or stronger or faster or better-connected than the hero. In most groups of buddies you'll find that each of them has a distinct personality and distinct traits and that they bring unique skills, experience, and knowledge that the hero will need to lean on in order to succeed. Alongside this they will each have a different viewpoint to the hero, helping him to evaluate options and make better decisions than he otherwise might if he were on his own. They act as moral compass and conscience, and the group is always bet-ter together than they are apart. Buddies are a good idea.

Sidekicks, on the other hand — well, frankly, I *hate* sidekicks — they're a bad idea.

Now don't get me wrong, occasionally they can be fun like Batman and Robin, The Lone Ranger and Tonto, The Green Hornet and Kato, but the problem with sidekicks is that in most cases they're not really necessary, and in a lot of cases they actually just get in the way or make unnecessary complications for the hero.

So why have them?

Well hold on and I'll come to that.

Buddies and sidekicks come in all shapes and sizes. They can be good or bad, brave or cowardly, dumb or smart, but they generally serve two purposes:

1) They give the hero someone to be with.

Seriously, they are the foil for almost all exposition, which is pretty much never a good thing. But in order to make your hero a bit more "human," they can come to his rescue when he's in trouble, they can provide the spark of inspiration that solves the mystery, and often they have skills or knowledge that the hero doesn't have. The other reason is....

2) They help the audience identify with your white knight.

Despite the flaws you've given your hero, the wound that makes them perfect for this story, your hero is often too good to be true. They want to do the right thing, they're brave, uncompromising, loyal. As an audience we need someone else — someone a bit more like us — to be around, and we can identify with the hero through the eyes of the sidekick.

Typically they come in four varieties:

1) Assistant
2) Best Friend
3) Brains
4) Muscle

The **Assistant** can literally be an assistant — like Alfred the butler in Batman — but they can also be an apprentice or a mentor or just a go-to guy. Whichever, they all have one thing in common. They don't fight. They can be the conscience, the sounding board, they can encourage or admonish, they are loyal and will keep secrets, but they don't get involved in the fight. That's something the hero must do for himself.

The **Best Friend** often represents something of the hero's former life, a touchstone if you like. They are the person who keeps the hero grounded. They are there when needed, come what may, and no matter how big the hero gets, the Best Friend always treats them the same, never kowtows, never disdains. Occasionally they will fight alongside the hero, occasionally they provide help in other ways, but they are the one person the hero can always count on.

A counterpoint to the brawn the hero usually displays, the **Brains** are usually content to stay away from anything physical, using their smarts to help the hero overcome the bad guys. It's not unusual for the two of them to be in different locations, the Brains guiding the hero remotely. Brains and brawn are two sides of the same coin and in many ways neither of these two would be successful as a soloist, but they make a great duet.

The **Muscle** is the fighting sidekick to a hero with brains, the shoot-first-ask-questions-later type. They are rarely apart because the brains can't go and save the day without the Muscle to back him up, but they do occasionally separate, allowing the Muscle to come in and save the day when the hero gets into trouble. Often depicted as kind of dumb or of limited ambition, the Muscle is happy to let the hero take the credit.

One thing that's important to bear in mind is that any of these buddies or sidekicks can be played for laughs, making them double as the **Comedy Relief.** They can still have their primary role, still do all of the things that we've mentioned, but they do them while cracking jokes, worrying about their own safety, teasing the hero and generally behaving inappropriately. It's also possible to have more than one of each in a group, although one will be the primary and the other will be secondary, and it's also possible, though rare, for any of the group to have their own Best Friend, Assistant, Brains, or Muscle, but only one; beyond that the group dynamic gets very complicated.

So why do I dislike sidekicks?

Well they're a double-edged sword (or double-ended lightsabre) because a really good sidekick is much more interesting than the main character. Let me explain. As I've already mentioned, the main character is too good to be true. He may be flawed in some way or wounded by something in his past, but he's basically a decent person, and even if you make him a gambling addict, a womaniser, scared of guns, or riddled with guilt over some past folly, we know he's going to do the right thing. But a sidekick, well he can do what he wants. He can cheat and lie and steal. He can do the dirty work that the hero won't do and line his pockets at every opportunity, he can be a bully or a pimp or a psychopath and practice any kind of degenerate behaviour you can imagine. The sidekick can be smarter than the hero, be an incredible shot with a gun, a master craftsman, a superb tracker, or that hoary old chestnut the gifted computer hacker, but none of it will matter because he's not the hero. What it does do, however, is make them really interesting characters. With all of this, your sidekick could also have a significantly bigger development arc than your hero, and if they change so much that they step in, help the hero, and save the day, then the audience will love the sidekick... and you will completely undermine your hero.

So here's the thing, if you really want to write a great main character, make the hero and the sidekick one and the same. Don't let your main character be black or white, don't even let them be shades of grey. Have them veer violently back and forth through all three. Make them nice one day, nasty the next. Have them smile and laugh with people, then go home and drink themselves senseless. Make them a thief and a bully who adores his children. Let them cuss out their superiors and then buy flowers for their Mum. What I'm trying to say is make them human. If a character is interesting enough to be a great sidekick, then they're probably interesting enough to be the main character.

Having said all that, if you must have a sidekick, then remember these immutable laws:

1) Make them a partner and not a distraction — permanently clueless, screaming sidekicks are just plain annoying, and no one will thank you.

2) Have them there for a reason — if all they do is stand next to the hero, then they don't need to be there, give them things to do on their own.

3) Give them skills and knowledge the hero does not have — make them useful and productive so they can help to move the story forward.

4) Make them contrasting personalities — remember, opposites attract. If your hero and sidekick are basically the same, then they will be boring together.

FAMILY, FACTIONS, FRICTION, AND FOES

Family

Family can mean many things. Any close-knit group can act like a family with each other — ask anyone whose ever been in the armed forces, or been a firefighter or police officer, or in a football team or street gang. But in this case I'm talking about the obvious and immediate family: fathers and mothers, brothers and sisters, husbands and wives, sons and daughters, grandparents, aunts, uncles, and cousins, and everything else in-between.

The family that kicks butt together, stays together. (*The Incredibles*, 2004)

The questions you have to ask when constructing a family are "What is the relationship like with the hero?" and "What is the relationship like with the other family members?" Basic questions, like:

1) Do they love or hate each other?
2) Are they affectionate or distant?
3) Are they encouraging and supportive or discouraging and unsupportive?
4) Are they proud of the hero or ashamed of the hero?

And don't forget the qualifier to each of these questions — WHY? It's no good just knowing that the father hates the uncle, you need to understand WHY they do and the answers to these questions will lay the basic groundwork for the relationship. Now let's dig a little deeper. Take each of your family members in turn and ask more searching questions.

Think about that family member's background.
1) Were they always around or were they away?
   a. If they were away, then where were they? At war? On business? In prison?
2) How did they treat the hero?
   a. Well? Badly? Indifferently? In what way? (Spoiled with gifts, bullying and abusive, or simply ignoring them.)
3) How did they treat their other family members?
   a. Well? Badly? Indifferently? In what way? (Spoiled with gifts, bullying and abusive, or simply ignoring them.)
4) What kind of person were they then?
5) How have they changed?

By forming an answer to each question, you start to deepen each character's relationship with the hero as well as set the foundations of the entire family dynamic. As you answer, go back to your hero and ask:
1. How do these things affect the hero's outlook?
2. Do they colour his behaviour to others, especially his own family?
3. Does he resent the other person or has he forgiven them?
4. Does the rest of the family know about this and do they understand it?

A word of warning
The list of questions you can ask may be endless and I personally shy away from full character biographies. They're the kind of "busy work" that helps a writer to procrastinate and not have to actually write, but it can help shape your character if you know whether they were popular at school or work, if they were bullied or not, if they were ever very ill, if they lost a loved one, and so on. So go as deep as you feel you need to

in order to fully draw out your character, but don't overthink this stuff; you only need to know as much as it takes to write your screenplay.

Factions and Friction

Factions can come in any shape, size, or species. (*Planet of the Apes*, 1968)

Once you have sketched-out your family group, you can start dividing them into factions. Factions are groups of people banded together for a common goal, most often to gain power over other factions in order to advance their own agenda, which generally means ruling over the world you have built and ultimately the wealth that comes with those positions of power. As I said earlier, family does not have to mean blood relatives, it can mean any close-knit group that is thrust together for extended periods of time, and factions are a great way of creating tension in any story that involves an establishment group such as the military, government, corporations, scientific communities, or ruling elite. They can also represent the two sides of your moral argument or your theme. Be very careful, however, about making it a simple black and white, good versus evil situation — life is rarely that straightforward.

Here's a quick exercise for you:

1) Pick the group within your larger family and decide what it is they want. Now choose which other group within your larger family they need to align with to achieve this aim. Now, why have they chosen to align with each other? What is group two's incentive to align with group one? Assuming they're successful, who ultimately will get to rule?

2) Now look at the opposing faction and figure out what route through <u>that</u> faction the path to success will have to take. Who in that group can be bought? Who can be manipulated? Who can be exiled? Who needs to be seduced? Which members cannot be corrupted in any way and must be eliminated? Plotting the downfall of a group you despise is fun, isn't it?

Don't forget that there will almost always be a matriarchal or patriarchal figure that — officially or unofficially — leads the group. There will be a mentor or voice-of-reason to confide in and who offers advice and guidance. Often there will be a detractor who seeks only to bring the leader down. Remember also that within each faction there will be those who actually like people on the opposite side and who are where they are through birth or circumstance, so pick one or two in each group who are outsiders, people you wouldn't normally expect to take that particular side.

There may also be other factions that are happy with the status quo, preferring to do nothing but just let things take their course, and there could be fourth or fifth factions that want something else entirely. It makes things much more interesting for the audience if they don't really know who to trust and gives the writer a great opportunity to lay red herrings and false trails. It also opens the story up for betrayals and surprise loyalties. Be cautious, though; the more complex these factions become, the more complex your story will ultimately be and harder to follow, so be careful not to overplay it.

Foes
At this point you should be starting to see how your plot can come together based on your "family dynamic" but the most important thing to

figure out is that someone amongst these groups is the foe. The villain. The bad guy. This person loathes your hero and wants him to fail. If your hero is one of the group leaders, then it could easily be one of the group outsiders working to undermine them. Conversely, if your hero is a low man on the totem pole, then it could easily be someone in a position of power in the group that he needs to defeat. But in any genre, the foe is always more interesting if no one around them suspects them of wrongdoing and, if you want to really connect with your audience on an emotional level, make the foe someone close to them that they would never suspect, someone with whom the hero shares a history.

Be careful who you trust. (*Minority Report,* 2004)

A strong bad guy is the engine of conflict and will help to drive the story forward. Without him the hero has no one to overcome and cannot be a hero. Once again, there are complete books dedicated to writing the perfect villain, but there are a few things to bear in mind:

1) How does the villain fit into the overall story?
   Is he simply someone who stands between the hero and his goal, the catalyst that forces the hero to change? Or is he bigger than that? Does he represent one whole side of the moral argument? Knowing this will tell you where in the "family" hierarchy he sits.

2) How does your hero fit into the villain's life?
   A truly memorable villain is always vastly more powerful, smarter, and has better resources than the hero, so how are they different? How are they the same? In what ways do they clash? Why is this villain the right villain for your hero?

3) How bad is your bad guy?
The villain is usually some reflection of the hero, so he needs to be credibly bad. A lone journalist is unlikely to go up against a ruthless and amoral warlord, slaughtering his way across a planet, but he might investigate an arms deal that brings down a corrupt regime.

4) What made him a villain?
Was it nature or nurture? Was he always a petty criminal, even as a child, and it just escalated as he got older? Was he brought up to act this way by parents or by a society for whom this is how life is lived? Or was there a traumatic incident such as seeing his parents butchered by a madman that tipped him over the edge? Importantly, how is this behaviour, experience, or incident reflected by the hero.

5) What does your villain love?
It doesn't have to be a person or pet — in fact, often it's better if it isn't, as it offers a vulnerability that the hero might take advantage of. But it could be a hobby, like growing roses or collecting antique vases, or baking cakes. The important thing is, it humanises the bad guy a little. Remember, the bad guy is always the hero of his own story.

6) What is your villain afraid of?
Everybody is afraid of something. It could just be that he's afraid of the hero — prophecy stories often centre around this — or it could be something egotistical, like fear of mediocrity or of not being respected. It could also be less tangible, like fear of the dark or of spiders, but make it credible, believable, and above all, relevant to the story.

7) Does your bad guy redeem himself?
At the end of the story, does he repent or does he stay a bad guy? If he does redeem himself then you need to plant that seed at the beginning of your story; avoid a sudden and random change of character; especially if he saves the hero.

Finally, your hero doesn't have to win and your bad guy doesn't have to lose. I know that's not the Hollywood way, but it can often be more interesting, and science fiction stories have a rich tradition of showing the effects of wanton hubris on both sides.

HUMAN CHARACTERS

I often hear that to truly write great characters you must know them forwards, backwards, and sideways; their childhood, their school years, their college years, first love, religious beliefs, how the character feels about their siblings, their parents, their extended family, colleagues, friends, and so on. Human characters in science fiction are every bit as complex, nuanced, and difficult to write well as human characters in any other genre. We touched on some of these elements for building your characters and their personality at the beginning of this chapter, and there are enough specialised books out there in the world to help you go further. But given science fiction's use of allegory to point to ourselves and discuss subjects that are often difficult to talk about in other ways, it's important that we cover some of the distinctively Sci-Fi subjects that won't get looked at anywhere else.

As you dig into the details of your world and figure out the culture, the religion, the morals and ethics, the occupations, and so on, you'll start to get details that will colour the attitudes, values, and emotions of your characters. In some cases this will form backstory that the audience will never see or hear about, and in other cases it will add to their physiology or psychology and establish personality and behaviour. In both cases it will manifest itself in the trivial details of the character's life. How your character folds his shirts, or how he keeps his desk tidy, the things that make him angry or sad or frustrated are the small details that will make him seem so much more real to an audience. Cultivate these things; they will stand you in good stead.

Stereotypes

Always ask yourself "Why does this character have to be in this story? What is their purpose?" Knowing this is the key to writing a memorable and successful character, not just for the hero or the villain — in some ways they're the easiest to answer for — but for the supporting players who need properly defined roles (otherwise they're just taking up space). We're all used to seeing the strong male hero rescue the damsel-in-distress, or fight his way out of a tough spot using guile and ingenuity while a lissom female screams along beside him, but these days it's not unusual to see a strong female character in science fiction and we have Warrant Officer Ellen Ripley to thank for that. However there are several stereotypes in science fiction, as in all genres, and I'm sure you know them:

The Alpha Male — handsome, brave, physically strong, works hard and plays harder, able to make tough decisions and live by them, willing to die for the cause, proud and uncompromising. We don't see too many of these kinds of guys anymore, maybe because we don't have as many Schwarzeneggers and Stallones anymore, but more likely because they're too good to be true and no one can relate to those guys in the modern world.

They don't come much more alpha than Jack O'Neil (Kurt Russell). (*Stargate*, 1994)

The All-Action Girl — simply the female version of the Alpha Male but in a skimpier or more revealing costume, a female character who is tough, strong, and a skilled fighter, but usually with some smarts to make up for any lack of physical strength and an empathy with her enemy that an Alpha Male will not demonstrate. Done well she'll be central to the plot, not a support act; done poorly she'll be "just one of the guys."

The Nerdy Guy — they're portrayed as weak, incompetent, not very attractive, often with some kind of physical or mental impediment, and always the third-wheel in a love triangle between the hero and the girl. They're the hero's sidekick, and you know how I feel about sidekicks.

The Best Girl Friend — she's the counter to the Nerdy Guy but not as unattractive — if only she'd take off those glasses! She's sweet, reliable, the companion, the shoulder to cry on, the homemaker and bookworm, the one the All-Action Girl borrows a dress from when she wants to look "girlie."

The Nice Normal Guy — we're seeing more and more of these guys in films and TV. Handsome but doesn't know it, fit but not physically strong, he's smart and good at his interesting job, he dresses well, is clean shaven and smells good — I'd say metrosexual, but he's not that self-aware — though he is caring and sharing and nice to be around, in touch with his feminine side without being effeminate.

The Sassy Best Friend — the female equivalent of the Nice Normal Guy, we don't see too many of these in science fiction, but they do exist. They're the bachelor girl, smart and funny, sexually fulfilled without needing commitment, educated, independent, and utterly self-aware.

I point these stereotypes out only because *I want you to avoid them like the plague!* They're old and hackneyed and have had their day in the sun. Do better than this. If you must use these stereotypes, and they do have their place in the world, then do your best to subvert them. Write a Nerdy Guy who can kill with a samurai sword or an All-Action Girl that collects My Little Pony figures, write not just with shades of grey, but in extremes of black and white that veer wildly. Above all, don't be boring.

Gender roles
The theme of gender and gender roles has been explored over and over in science fiction and you will find no other genre as open to its discussion. We're used to seeing a reversal of the stereotypical gender roles of strong man and weak woman, especially in science fiction TV shows with the likes of Olivia Dunham in *Fringe*, Starbuck in *Battlestar Galactica*, Sam Carter in *Stargate-SG1*, Kathryn Janeway in *Star Trek: Voyager*, and back to Susan Ivanova in *Babylon 5*, but it's a lot less usual to see the use of single gender or occasionally non-gender societies, where science fiction is happy to question the common perceptions of its audience.

The smartest lady in the FBI. Special Agent Olivia Dunham (Anna Torv). (*Fringe* [TV], 2008)

In her 1969 novel *The Left Hand of Darkness*, Ursula K. Le Guin created a planet, Gethen, populated by humans of a single gender who, during the mating season, spontaneously adopted one gender or the other. Since the same person can be father to one child and mother to a different child, there are no typical gender roles; everyone raises the children and everyone goes out to work. This creates a society that purports to offer the best traits of human nature, and the social order supports that.

While this example is from a book rather than a film, it does serve to point out that you can think differently about gender if you put your mind to it, and like much of science fiction, changed gender roles can add real depth to the layers of your world-building.

Sexual orientation

Like gender roles, the standard ideas of sexual orientation are easily subverted in science fiction, but far more so in fiction than in films. While TV has been more adventurous with the sexual orientation of its characters over the last few years, reflecting the diversity and complexity of contemporary society, it's probably just as difficult to sell a tentpole science fiction film with a gay or lesbian main character today as it was 50 years ago. But at least gay and lesbian characters are far more commonplace now — even if they still can't be the hero. But once again, there are other ways to approach the idea of different sexual roles in science fiction, and it's worth noting one or two.

In 1972 Isaac Asimov published *The Gods Themselves*, in which our sun is made unstable by an alien life form from a parallel universe with different physical laws to ourselves. This renders them almost made of gas and they consume material from our sun to convert into energy. Described as "Soft Ones," they are comprised of three sexes; Rationals (logical, scientific, masculine) who provide the sperm, Emotionals (intuitive, feminine) who provide the energy needed to procreate, and Parentals (masculine) who bear the children and raise them. During sex the different sexes "melt" together physically, and as the "melt" becomes total the Rational impregnates the Parental while the Emotional provides the energy.

The point here is not to subvert for the sake of subversion; there has to be a proper reason for any of these things to be different and it must always be in service to the story. But it pays to try and think differently. Move outside of your and your audience's comfort zone and push radical ideas and notions whenever you can. If everything in your science fictional world is the same as down here on Earth, then your writing will not be all it can be.

A quick word about names
Choosing the right name for your characters is tough, but very important. It needs to be descriptive, revealing something of the character themselves, their age, their place and status, and yet not so on-the-nose that it's ludicrous. And it needs to be unique, not just from the other characters in the film, but from characters you have seen or heard before so it has a chance to live beyond your movie.

Here are a few top tips for naming names:

1) Choose names that reflect personality. If he's a sneak, call him Jack Sly; if he's a coward, call him Paul Runner; if he's always trying to please, call him Tim Eager. These are a bit on-the-nose, but you get the idea. Don't make any name too long, keep them

simple, easy to say, and easy to remember — just use a thesaurus when doing your own!

2) Choose names that reflects the character's role. It's amazing how many times a murderer is called Cain, or Kane, or Kayne. The symbolism there is obvious. But you could call your mentor character Wiseman, or you could call the new girl Dawn. In my screenplay, *Outpost One*, the main character has to guide a group of people away from danger, so I called him Shepherd.

3) Make it age-appropriate. Old folk are not called Pepper or Meadow or Drew (unless the film is set 100 years in the future), and conversely youngsters are not called Delores or Enid or Ruth unless there's a fashion for old names and that'd be hard to explain in a film. While we're here, make it appropriate to period, status, locale and ethnicity. Young, white lawyers in London are not generally called Winston unless they have an outstanding origin story and in 1740 they would not only have had a traditional name like William or Jonathan, they would have been rare.

4) Combine the common and the unusual. Try a common first name with an unusual surname, or vice versa. Try Paul Testament or Colt Smith or Derek Bastard. Luke Skywalker is a great example of this.

5) Don't give people similar names. Avoid having Jack, Jeff, Jim, and John all in the same group. It's confusing for the reader and often for the writer, too. Also avoid names that collide, like John and Jovan, which may sound different but look the same on the page. Also avoid Craig and Greg, which don't just look the same, they sound the same as well.

6) If you're writing names for humans on another planet, make them similar but different to names from Earth. Try Yohn instead of John, or Isbeth instead of Elizabeth, and allow them their own cultural differences. For example, people brought up in an environment of war will likely have strong, warrior-like names. Avoid cute spellings though; Chloe is fine, but Khlowye

is just silly, so don't do it. While we're on the subject, if you're naming a race of aliens, make them different but not confusing. Names like Xyxinyzc are ridiculous, unpronounceable, and don't do anyone any favours, so avoid them. Use simple names — even single-word names — that are easy to remember and easy to say.

A final word and one that I read somewhere. Avoid names that end with the letter S. It's a small thing, but names that end in the letter S are hard to write and hard to read in the possessive form so it's just easier to avoid using them.

Non-Human Characters — How Alien is Alien?

The notion of "The Other"

Science fiction has always been fascinated by the notion of "The Other" — meaning something different from the norm, something unusual or strange, something distasteful to us, something alien. But alien doesn't have to mean "creature from another planet." It can just as easily mean from somewhere different that we don't know or understand. Remember, the term used for a person living in a country illegally is still an "alien." When writing alien characters, it's important, if they're going to be convincing, to understand and exploit this notion of The Other and to express it in things that we truly will never understand.

Unsurprisingly, John Carter (Taylor Kitsch) is way more interested in Dejah Thoris (Lynn Collins) than Tars Tarkas (Willem Defoe). (*John Carter,* 2012)

Just like us

Without naming names, one of my pet peeves about science fiction is that all of the alien species that inhabit the various universes are hominid in nature. They have two arms, two legs, two eyes, a nose, a mouth, and presumably one set of sexual organs and one place to excrete from. In other words, they're just like us. Except for that weird wrinkly forehead, or the pointy ears or the nose thing. Now there is a school of thought that says that this is highly likely. In any world where life exists it's hard to see any kind of evolution taking place that isn't Darwinian in nature, and thus creatures with two or more legs, two forward-facing eyes, two good ears — predators in fact — will be the dominant species.

But isn't that just boring?!

I know we can be constrained by budgets and union rules, but is that the best we can do? Really? A man in a rubber suit or with a prosthetic nose is the height of science fiction sophistication? Please!

And this expands out to other things as well, like greeting them in English and them being able to understand and reply with no issues because there was some kind of translator gizmo in his ear, conveniently forgetting to explain how a previously unknown language was programmed into the translator gizmo to start with.

You cannot dress a human up in a rubber suit and call them alien, no one will believe you and you will look foolish. You may, however, want to keep certain humanoid elements so that your audience can identify with your creatures — for example, having eyes helps us focus where we look and helps our alien to express emotion.

Why have aliens at all?

Good question, and it goes back to why we write science fiction. Alien creatures allow us to hold a mirror up to ourselves and explore what it means to be human. Aliens help us to show the importance of our humanity, our ability to nurture, to love, to compromise, to show loyalty and have faith, and to make deep emotional connections — uniquely human qualities that we can be reminded of through alien eyes.

Alien races can also act as a stand-in for just about anything that we want to criticise but cannot easily point at directly. Aliens let us discuss issues of gender, race, religion, bigotry, oppression, hatred, and so on, but without preaching to our audience. No one wants to be harangued for two hours about the morals and ethics of apartheid, but they'll watch an alien species caught up in a South African township and they'll empathise when a human exposed to their biotechnology starts to metamorphosise into one of them.

Wikus Van De Merwe (Sharlto Copley) lays down the law. (*District 9,* 2009)

We can also use aliens in comedy settings to show the absurdity of human life, the silliness of the things we hold dear, and the day-to-day rituals we observe at work and at home to preserve some semblance of status, when really it's our friends and family we should be most concerned with.

That's a lot to consider, so how do we go about writing great aliens? First of all, ask yourself why you have aliens. Are they really necessary to your story, or could another human work just as well? If you take a long hard look at your alien characters and find that the story would work just as well if they were human, then you don't need them to be alien. Change them. Try using another human but one that thinks in a totally different and alien way to your other characters and to your audience. Your story will be better for it and your message will resonate more with your audience.

If you are going to have an alien character in your film, then you need to take it seriously. It must be believable and it must feel real. The best thing about writing alien characters is that there are no rules. Seriously, you can write whatever you want. Entirely new species are at your fingertips and they can be any size, any colour, any shape you please. But, as with all writing, there are guidelines you should be aware of.

Creating an alien species
First, let's have a quick look at the laws of nature.

The universe is governed by fundamental laws of nature, and they are absolutely unbreakable. Everything that exists within the universe is, ultimately, controlled by these laws. That includes the human body, which is governed by the laws of physics and chemistry.

Now I'm being simplistic here, but our weight depends on gravity and our weight in any given location depends upon our mass, that's why we weigh one-sixth of our Earth weight when we're on the moon for the same mass. We also occupy a certain amount of space (some of us more than others... ahem!) and we exist for a certain length of time — infant to child to adult to elderly person — while existing in certain physical states (solid, liquid, gas).

No matter what, organic bodies conform to these laws of physics.

Now let's have a quick lesson in human physiology.

The human body functions at three general levels. **Molecular**; the molecule being the basic functional entity of a human. **Cellular**; groups of cells working together as tissues, different tissues collecting together forming organs, and groups of organs performing together called systems. Finally we have **Regional**; specific organs working together as a unit, like hands that we use to grip things. What is immediately apparent here is that there is a distinct and unbreakable relationship between the structure and the functions of the human body. And while there is undoubtedly tremendous variation among humans, each structure is designed to perform a particular function and each function requires particular structures with which to perform.

Isn't that cool!

Our bodies are amazing in lots of other incredible ways. We have evolved a supporting structure so we can stand and we use several types of bio-mechanical machines in the form of levers, pulleys, and valves in a mechanical arrangement so we can operate the structures, but also move the entire body around from place to place. We also constantly carry on a series of functions known as life processes. For instance, we consume materials for energy, growth, and repair through nutrition, we reproduce so human life can continue, and all of this is controlled by hormones which monitor body chemistry and the nervous system which works like a printed circuit board carrying signals from system to system.

So how do we apply this thinking to our aliens?
Well what your aliens look like is also going to be governed by these laws of physics and lessons in physiology. Whether they're tiny furry rodents or gigantic hairless apes or 7-foot-long worms that live underground, they will have evolved in ways that we can understand. They will have a particular size and weight, a skeletal structure that supports them, a set of bio-mechanical machinery that they use to move around and do stuff, and a series of life processes that help them live and reproduce. When you're describing your aliens, make sure that you take these things into account and don't prescribe characteristics to them that don't make any sense in the real world.

For example, if your aliens need to be 12 feet tall, then, based on human proportions, they should also have correspondingly thicker bones and be much heavier in weight, but they wouldn't be that much stronger because of the extra weight being carried around. They are also likely to move more slowly and need to consume much more food to keep up their energy. However, if they had arrived on Earth and our gravity was much less than theirs, then they might feel much lighter and their extra strength could possibly enable them to easily jump 50 feet in the air.

I'm not suggesting here that you do the exact math, although you can if you're feeling up to it. But use common sense to ensure that your aliens feel authentic.

Other factors
There are other factors, of course, that go into the creation of an alien species. Worlds that are covered in ice and snow will evolve creatures that are covered in fur with thick layers of fat to help keep out the cold.

Planets that are hot, arid, and desert-like will evolve creatures that are dark-skinned and able to survive for long periods without water, and if your planet's environment fluctuates wildly or has distinct seasons, then your aliens may migrate to other parts of the world during those seasons. All creatures will communicate in some way, whether through actual speech or from more animalistic sounds, and the more complex the group, the more complex the speech is likely to be. If they are a race of bugs they may well have a hive mind and a single queen.

Just as our own physiology has evolved from ecological need, so should that of our aliens. For an alien race to effectively mirror or act as a counter to our own, then they should be just as richly and accurately developed. Posing a few questions to yourself before you start to write will help you understand just how physically different your aliens can and should be and then start to raise basic questions about their attitudes to each other and to us, the alien species in their world.

Here are 20 basic questions to ask when thinking about alien creatures:

1) Do they come from a hot or cold planet?
2) Is the environment hostile?
3) Do they have extremes of environment, such as snowy mountains or arid deserts?
4) What is the gravity like on their home planet?
5) Do they have tides affected by a moon or moons?
6) Do they have a single sun and how does it affect the atmosphere?
7) How do they breath?
8) Do they have speech?
9) What is their skin like?
10) What colour are they?
11) Do they have eyes, ears, a mouth? How many, and where?
12) Do they live underground or in trees or in buildings?
13) What do they eat?
14) How do they get food? Do they grow or gather or hunt?
15) What other creatures live there?
16) Do they fear predators?

17) Have they suffered extinction events like an ice age?
18) How do they get around? Do they walk or fly or jump?
19) Compared to humans, are they tall or short, fat or thin?
20) Are they inherently loud and aggressive, or shy and quiet?

Thinking About Viewpoint

Whose point of view do you choose?
One of the first decisions you have to make is whose point of view (POV) you are going to tell your story through. Now usually this is straightforward; it'll be the main character's POV because it's their story. But that's not always the case. What happens if the main character is not in the scene? Well in that case it'll be whichever of your characters the scene is centred around — unless that character dies, in which case the scene needs to unfold from the POV of someone who witnesses the death.

The other time you may want to see a different POV is if you want to show the main character through the eyes of someone else in the story. This is especially true if you're telling your story through flashback or with some kind of omniscient narrator, but in the case of an alien race it may be that a change of viewpoint can really amplify the differences — or similarities — between them and their human counterparts.

Either way there are a couple of mistakes that a lot of writers make when trying to establish a viewpoint for a scene. The most common is to make the camera — or reader — a static viewer of the scene when what you really want is for them be an active participant. Here's an example of a static camera scene:

```
Joe picks up the gun and points it at Melody. We
see his hands shake and he looks confused. He
shouts at her.

                    JOE
          What did you do to me?
          I thought we would be together.
          Why?
```

Melody laughs at Joe and we can see his eyes are
glazing over. He's feeling dizzy and he can barely stand.

                    MELODY
          Stay with you? Forever, together.
          You're a loser Joe. Always have
          been, always will be.

Joe cannot keep his arm raised and drops the gun.
The last thing he hears before passing out is her
laughter and the clip of her heels as she leaves.

You see what I mean. It sounds like someone is watching the scene
unfold and is describing everything that happens as they watch. Now
let's try the scene again but with a more active point of view.

Hands shaking, eyes glazing over, Joe's breathing is shallow as he tries to draw a dead bead on
Melody.

                    JOE
          What did you do to me?
          I thought we would be together.
          Why?

Melody's laughter slices through him, his breath
more ragged as she barks.

                    MELODY
          Stay with you? Forever, together.
          You're a loser Joe. Always have
          been, always will be.

Waves of nausea wash over Joe and his trembling
hand drops the gun, Melody's heels on the cold
tiles the last thing he hears before oblivion
takes him.

See the difference? The second version, while not the greatest writing in the world admittedly, is much more involving for the reader, putting them inside Joe's viewpoint so they feel the scene rather than just see it. Joe doesn't just hear her laugh, it *slices through him*. Your writing will feel much more visceral, more emotionally engaging, if you make the camera a participant and not just a recorder.

So how does this change for science fiction? Well in essence it won't, but if your viewpoint character happens to be an alien or non-human character, then their viewpoint will be skewed according to their social and cultural background. What we see as hostile or barbaric or affectionate may be seen completely differently by an alien, and their reactions and attitudes will vary accordingly. Imagine the movie *Alien* seen through the eyes of the Alien? Or *Predator* from the viewpoint of the Predator? This is a difficult idea to pull off, and probably the main reason why alien viewpoint characters are as rare as hen's teeth, but I'll wager that if someone could get it right, then it would make a really fascinating story.

EXERCISE THREE

Lets go back to the news item we looked at in the last exercise.

In my infinite wisdom (!) I've decided to transplant this story to a recently discovered planet that, as far as current technology can tell, is inhabited only by simple microbes and bacteria. The atmosphere on this planet, while not completely hostile to human life, can be made far more habitable for the incoming colonists by terraforming.

An advance party have set, in geostationary orbit around the planet, several satellite-like devices that serve two purposes:

1) They house giant mirrors which reflect light and heat from a nearby sun onto the surface, triggering strategically placed "factories" to emit tonnes of greenhouse gases, heating the atmosphere and mimicking the process of photosynthesis that plants use to turn carbon dioxide into oxygen.

2) They also provide an early warning system for the colonists, alerting them to incoming craft, and sentry/security duties, having been weaponised to protect them from potential aggressors.

With an Earth election looming, the President of United Earth Peoples has decided to perform the inaugural switching-on of the terraforming technology personally, and will be on-planet along with several spectacularly rich financial backers who wish to see and be seen. Unfortunately for them, some activists protesting against "humanity playing God" have hacked the satellites. They see terraforming as favouring only human interests — particularly financial interests — to the detriment of the natural ecology, and are sworn to protect the existing native life-forms at all costs. To this end they have decided to make examples of the colonists, the President, and the financiers by killing them with their own technology, in front of a live TV audience for maximum political gain. However, there is an 8-hour window before the live TV hook-up will come into operation, so that's how long the people on the planet have to save themselves.

Okay, now we need some characters. So work out:

1) Who is your hero, and why that guy?
2) Does he have a sidekick or partner?
   a. Tell us about him.
3) Are there buddies around him?
   a. Tell us about them.
4) Is there a love interest?
   a. Who and why?
5) What are the factions amongst each group?
   a. The President and his entourage.
   b. The Financiers and their people.
   c. The Activists.
6) Who has the most influence in each group, technically and in reality?
7) Who is in charge of the situation?
   a. Is it the hero?
   b. Is it someone else?
   c. Are they at loggerheads with the hero?
8) Who is the villain?
   a. Why is she the villain?
   b. What does she stand to gain?

And so on. Keep going until you have created a full cast of characters. Use what you've learned from this chapter and get them written down. If you don't want to do an exhaustive list, just concentrate on the four or five key characters.

Extra Credit

We start to talk about plotting in the next chapter, but you can kick-start the process by looking at each of your characters in turn and asking yourself "What's the worst thing that can happen to this person in this situation?" and "What's the best thing that can happen to this person in this situation?" The resulting answers can be used to power your initial plot elements.

CHAPTER FOUR

PLOTTING

TURNING AN IDEA INTO A STORY

Most stories are about characters who have to fight for very high stakes against very long odds, whether they're saving the world from giant asteroids or galvanising the human race to fight invading alien hordes. But win or lose, the key to making your audience laugh with them, scream for them, and feel an emotional connection with them is the stuff that happens along the way, the obstacles they have to overcome. In other words, the plot. I can't help you to write a plot, but I can help you with some exercises to help build one and point out some mistakes to avoid along the way, so here goes.

A brief word about structure:

The Beginning
Rule number one, don't be boring. If you have to explain the entire history of your world and set up your main character before you can get started, you've already lost the reader. This means keep the backstory to yourself until it's time to reveal it, and even then, only in small doses. It is generally accepted wisdom that you should start a scene as late as you possibly can and end it as quickly as you possibly can and that's the best advice you'll ever get on writing beginnings.

The Middle
The middle is not a space filler. The middle is where you throw rocks at your protagonist. Obstacle after obstacle needs to come her way, each one getting harder and tougher than the previous one until we reach the climactic ending. During this time of "rising conflict" the external obstacles will open our hero up to reveal her own inner conflict, the wound, or ghost from her past that is stopping her from growing and changing

as a human being, and it is in overcoming these physical obstacles that she will overcome her mental obstacles and triumph over the bad guy.

The End
Make sure your ending reaches a proper and satisfying conclusion. Loose ends should be wrapped up, set ups should be paid off, girls should be kissed and the themes and moral arguments of your story should be fully stated and reinforced. Either your main character will have changed and grown as a person, or else those around him will have changed and grown as a result of his actions. Whatever happens, you do not want the reader to be looking around to see if they lost the back page of your screenplay and missed something.

Useful tips
1) Know whose story you're telling and make that character as active as possible.
By far the biggest problem I see in screenplays is a passive main character who either doesn't do enough or isn't in enough jeopardy for me to really care about what happens. We've already mentioned this, but if the primary purpose of the plot is so that your main character can grow and change, then knowing your character and knowing how they will change by the end of the story will often help to build your plot.

2) Keep the structure strong.
Screenplay structure works and you need to use it. Don't view it as prison or a route to formulaic writing, but as a foundation you will build your own house upon. Don't skip steps, don't avoid setting things up and paying them off, don't race for the ending, don't force dialogue. It's there for a reason, so use it.

3) Have enough conflict.
Conflict, being the lifeblood of good storytelling, must flow through every scene. But it cannot be arbitrary, it must be directly connected to your protagonist's growth and change. If you're having second act problems, it'll be because your main character is weak and consequently there's not enough conflict driving your story.

4) Don't have too many characters.
Juggling lots of characters is like trying to juggle plates on sticks and

about as much fun. Not everything in your story needs a new character to say it or experience it, so wherever possible lose characters, combine them or kill them off. If they don't have a journey of their own to go on, then they needn't come along for the ride. If they are truly that interesting, then maybe they need their own story.

5) Don't slow down.
Every scene you write should either a) move the story forward, or b) reveal something of character. This means you need to cut every scene that doesn't do either of those two things. People standing around chatting is pretty boring to watch unless you can write dialogue like Kevin Smith or Quentin Tarantino, and you probably can't, so in order to keep the pace up and keep things moving, never have an extraneous scene in your movie.

BRAINSTORMING

Brainstorming exercises
You found your story and played the "What if..?" game, then figured out who your hero is and why that guy, and you know your villain and your supporting characters. Here are some more tools that you can use to figure out your plot.

1) Write a list of 50 things that could go wrong.
This is actually pretty hard to do. Anyone can sit down and write 20 things, maybe 25 at a push, but writing 50 takes some doing. They can be as mad or harebrained as you like, and believe me, when you run out of sensible options, that is all that's left, and the only rule is that you cannot give up and you must finish all 50. Once that's done you have a bunch of options to expand into your plot.

2) Figure out your ending as soon as possible.
No matter how cool your beginning might be, try to figure out your ending as soon as possible BEFORE you get going on the middle. One of the main reasons people run out of steam in the middle of a screenplay is that they don't know where they're going. Do yourself a favour, work out your ending first, then write towards it. You'll be amazed how much easier it is to get somewhere if you know where you're going.

3) Add genre layers to your idea.
You want to write a science fiction film and you have an idea but you may not be sure of the tone. Is it a drama or a thriller, a comedy or an action adventure film? Test your list of 50 things that could go wrong and see how they stack up when you add a layer from a second genre on top. If it falls short of ideas, then start writing a list of 50 comedy things that could go wrong, 50 horror things that could wrong, etc.

4) Mindmap your story ideas.
I've always been a big fan of mindmapping. Draw a circle in the centre of a large piece of paper and write your story idea in it. Then brainstorm around the idea by mindmapping all the things you can think of branching from that core idea.

5) Do some research.
Take the thing that spawned your story idea and go research it thoroughly. As you make notes and build a research folder for all this stuff, let your findings lead you wherever they may, be it an interesting character, a strange occupation, or an amazing location. You never know what this might turn up.

6) Get it down on paper.
If an idea stays in your head, then it's only an idea. Writing it down starts the process of turning it into a story. The same goes for a problem with the story. Putting it down on paper articulates the problem in a way that lets you start fixing it.

7) Move your scene locations.
If you're struggling with scenes, then try moving inside scenes to outside or day scenes to night. Try writing them in the rain or the snow or the baking sun. Try making a scientist meet at an illegal dog fight or an Armenian cab driver in a London gentlemen's club. It may not work, but it could spark the creativity needed to move you on.

8) Dissect another screenplay.
Find a screenplay from a film similar to your own and divide it up into scenes. Try to identify the conflict in each scene. Look for who is up against whom and what is at stake for each character. Make a note of the

plot points and how they relate to character change, and while you're at it, note the set-ups and pay-offs and how the structure holds up. Then look at your own screenplay and see how it compares. Find the gaps in your structure and, now that you have the materials, repair them.

9) How do the rules of your world change things?

If you're struggling with a story set in a very different world, how does it affect the story? Does stronger or weaker gravity have an impact? Does the environment have an impact? What about the way people dress or the attitude towards the sexes? Is the country at war? If we can make things move abnormally slow or fast, it can be used to increase tension in different ways.

10) List everything that won't happen.

If you can't figure out where your story might go next, start making a list of all the things that definitely won't happen next. This is a great exercise for unplugging the dam in your head and letting the ideas flood out. Surprisingly, the idea you need is often just under the surface somewhere.

11) Use images as triggers.

Browse the web, go to the library, visit a gallery, buy some books or magazines, and make an album or collage of all the images that hit you with immediate impact. They can be related to your story in terms of scenery of landscape or general appearance, or they can be character studies or portraits, but use them to inspire your plotting. Take specific details or elements and write them into your scenes or your character descriptions. Why are they there? What do they do? What is their significance?

12) Write the mundane details of your characters' lives.

Forget about your big event or story for the time being and think about what the characters would be doing if this wasn't happening. Would they be shopping, or travelling, or working in a zoo. Would they be in the military, or in a corporation, and where would they sit in the hierarchy? The mundane day-to-day details of your characters and their behaviours are often what sets them apart. This could be the trigger to a better story.

13) Try the rule of three.
I've heard it said a few times that it takes three good ideas to make a story work and this is where your clipping software and your notebooks come into their own. Rummage through them and find three things that you've marked or clipped or written and that will work together to make a story. It could be a location from one source and a technology from somewhere else and a character from a third place, but keep mixing and matching until you have something that works. Once again, it's really your subconscious that you're putting to work here as you try to trigger ideas for your film.

Sounds easy, right? But I find plotting probably the hardest part of any writing and I only managed to do it by employing these tools to help. Sometimes using one or two will be enough, other times I need all of them, but each is a useful thing to try when you're fleshing out that story.

WHAT ARE YOU TRYING TO SAY?

As we've already discussed, science fiction is the genre of allegory, allowing us to highlight big social concerns by telling stories rather than preaching messages. It does this by looking at three different aspects of our society:

1) People — through politics, law, religion, corporate greed, war, racism, population growth, etc.
2) Place — through climate change, pollution, deforestation, not enough space, not enough people, etc.
3) Technology — through genetic engineering, robotics, nanotech, disease control, communications, etc.

The simple and obvious way to approach these issues is to look at how they are affecting us now and extrapolate what the end result may be if things are allowed to go unchecked. But there is another way we can look at social change, and that's by looking at where our created-world society is in terms of its developmental stage (See Chapter Five).

When you look at the growth stages of society in this way it's easy to see how any one of them could be used to show how a change in People, Place, or Technology will impact things. But science fiction stories actually work best when they are set between the stages and show the effects of moving from one stage to the next. This is rich, fertile soil, because we already have a conflict between wanting new technologies and better education, and so on, and the downsides of overcrowding and the collapse of communities.

So what are you trying to say?

Well, in order to see a particular problem, you have to look at the whole system, and to change that problem you will have to change the whole system. This is the key insight you are trying to demonstrate. But in order to do that you have to have your own clear vision of how your world is and how your society can change and grow. You have to show that society needs to deal with these problems but also how they can do it without destroying everything that went before.

Despite the apocryphal nature of a lot of science fiction, there is usually a positive message. There's a promise that because the human race is tough and smart and resilient, we can fight our way through any adversity and emerge on the other side with our humanity intact, learning from our mistakes and moving on with a new measure of peace, understanding, and, above all, hope.

That's a big ask, and is the stuff of epic storytelling when it's done right.

ESTABLISHING THEME

Every story worth telling has a point in there somewhere. That "point" is the theme, and theme, as you're probably aware, is the central question that the writer is trying to explore in a screenplay. It's important to state that the theme is not the moral message implicit in the story, but that it's a much bigger concept upon which the entire foundation of the story rests. For example, in a story of revenge the moral message might be "Two wrongs don't make a right." It's universally understandable, but it's way too trite to be a theme. The theme will be a much bigger question such as "Can a man truly show forgiveness towards someone who has done him the ultimate wrong? " Now that's a theme!

Like the moral message of your story, your theme should appeal to a wide cross-section of people in many countries and from many cultures. The ideas you explore should be instantly recognisable and, as such, will always be implied in the writing rather than explicitly stated.

Neo (Keanu Reeves) tries hard to believe. (*The Matrix*, 1999)

The theme of *The Matrix* is something along the lines of "If you believe in yourself you can achieve anything." Throughout the film people constantly ask Neo if he believes. They tell him others believe in him. He argues that he doesn't want to believe what's happened. But no one ever actually says "If you believe in yourself you can achieve anything." During the dojo fight sequence Morpheus asks Neo if he believes his speed and strength has anything to do with his muscles inside the Matrix. When he visits the Oracle she tells him Morpheus believes in him, but she doesn't. It's not until Morpheus is kidnapped and Neo manages to rescue him that he finally realises that he has to believe in himself and when he does, he kicks Agent ass!

So you can use key words in dialogue to imply theme. *The Matrix* uses the word "believe" numerous times in dialogue throughout the screenplay, but it never actually states the theme out loud. That's for the audience to discover on their own. It's also worth remembering that a good director will be able to articulate the theme in ways that the writer cannot, such as through use of colours or numbers, costumes, locations, and by using the cinematic language of framing, lighting, *mise-en-scène*, and so on.

To be honest, I don't usually understand my own theme until I get to the end of a screenplay. I only have a notion of what it might be once I've read a finished draft. But when I do understand my theme, I go back and address it in every stage of the re-writes. Alongside character, plot, world and genre, theme is probably the most important element of your screenplay. If you can think about what it is you're trying to

74

say, what aspect of being human you're looking to explore, then those insights can inform all of your plot, character, and dialogue choices as you write; at the very least, it gives you a touchstone you can always go back to whenever you get stuck during the writing.

AVOIDING CLICHÉ

Cliché [klee'shey] noun
1. (in art, literature, drama, etc.) a trite or hackneyed plot, character trait or development, use of speech, colour, technology, musical expression, stereotype, etc. that has lost originality, ingenuity, and impact by long overuse.

The giant list of overused science fiction clichés is vast (really, try Googling it) and it is inevitable that at some stage you will resort to use of cliché to tell your story, whether deliberately through knowing comedy or satire, or by accident because you just weren't paying attention and ended up painting yourself into a corner. However, it's important to point out that not all clichés are created equal and their use is not always the kiss of death to your screenplay. What is important, however, is knowing that over-reliance on cliché is what signals the amateur from the professional, and thus the strong, original story from the plain, ordinary also-ran.

I'm assuming that, as a reader of this book, you are familiar with one or two science fiction films and you will recognise more than a few of the worst types of clichés, the ones that are so old and worn that they really should be locked in a darkened room, never again to see the light of day. They include:

- The villain, or one of his henchmen, travels back in time to kill the hero's mother before the hero is born.
- As the story resolves, it was all just a dream.
- A huge alien fits into the body of a human until the big climax where it suddenly becomes huge again.
- Scientists are always wacky eccentrics or moody geniuses, female scientists are always supermodels.
- The son of the chief of your alien tribe will be a rebel fighting the system, his daughter will be the most beautiful girl in the tribe.

But there are others, ones that even today, if used well and appropriately, and in the right context, will happily see you through a tough plot point. I still see things like:

- The countdown timer on a bomb or other doomsday device is stopped by the hero with just one second left to go.
- The ventilation shafts in a spaceship or building give easy and total access to the rest of the spaceship or building. The same goes for sewer networks in cities.
- The entire world of the story is dominated by huge corporations.
- The hero is a drunken ne'er-do-well (or similar) who sobers up in time to save the day.

And truthfully, despite the fact that they are old and hoary, I don't mind these kind of clichés if they make sense and if I'm wrapped up in the story, because everything else — characters, plot and so on — is good.

Then there are the third kind, the lazy ones. I see these more and more often, new clichés that defy all known scientific laws and all reasonable logic and common sense — these ones in particular you need to avoid. They include:

- Computer AIs that can hold down conversations and display emotions exactly like humans.
- During chase scenes, only the fat guy ever gets out of breath. Ever. And everyone else is prepared to just leave him behind.
- Every alien race knows all about the existence of other alien races, but bizarrely, if more than two humans find out, it'll be the end of the universe.
- Post-apocalyptic societies that have reverted back to feudalism.
- Post-apocalyptic societies that treat lost technology with almost holy reverence.
- Post-apocalyptic societies where every journey is a few days walk — all of the bicycles seem to have died as well.

You might have guessed I've got it bad for post-apocalyptic societies. I've yet to see one that is truly convincing, and they are trailblazers for all-new clichés.

The Thief (Michael Kenneth Williams) resorts to cliché. (*The Road*, 2009)

I think it's worth pointing out that, in and of themselves, clichés are not bad, they are just tools for writing like everything else, and if they work for the story and they make sense, then use them by all means. Having said that, if you can find a way to play around with a cliché and turn it into something different, then you can have some fun with your audience.

You can subvert a cliché by making it seem like the same old thing we all know and then turning it on its head. My all-time favourite example is in the film *Deep Blue Sea* when Russell Franklin (Samuel L. Jackson) is giving his big heroic speech to rally the troops and halfway through gets eaten by a shark. I've got to say I laughed out loud the first time I saw it.

You can also invert a cliché by taking the usual treatment and reversing it to play against expectations. Comedian Rich Hall has a hilarious song in this vein called "Do anything you want to the girl, just don't hurt me." I think that says it all.

As a coda, it is generally acknowledged that if a character, plot, or setting has been used in the *Star Trek* universe, it is tainted beyond the capacity for re-use at any time by anybody — even J. J. Abrams.

EXERCISE FOUR

Two exercises for the price of one here:

The news article from Exercise Two concerned a stolen laptop allowing thieves access to the codes that control the ISS, but imagine if former President Ronald Reagan had gone ahead with his "Strategic Defence Initiative" and the stolen codes were for a weaponised satellite that was in orbit around the Earth? This satellite can hit any target on Earth with an accuracy of +/- eighteen centimetres and the control codes are up for auction to the highest bidder.

Now this scenario brings us back to a fairly standard thriller set in a more-or-less contemporary USA, but I want to put a twist on it by saying that the plot needs to have two interconnected story threads:

1. In thread one, someone has to track down the criminals, take them out and recover the stolen codes before they are re-sold on the black market.

2. In thread two a crew of seven has to man a space shuttle, board the Master Satellite, and disable it in case the first team on the ground fails to locate the criminals.

Part One — brainstorm around those ideas, then write out some key story beats for this film. Incidentally, if you ever get it made, I'll be first in the queue to go see it!

Part Two — go back to the idea from Exercise Three, incorporate your characters and then brainstorm around how that story will pan out.

In both exercises remember to use the tools mentioned previously: 50 things that could go wrong, figure out your ending, add a genre layer, the rule of three, and so on.

Extra Credit
Think of a movie you really disliked. Now go through the story elements of that movie — the scenes, the characters, the plot — and write down how you would rearrange them or alter them so that it becomes a film you do like.

CHAPTER FIVE

BUILDING YOUR WORLD

DECIDING ON SETTING

Building a world for your characters to live in is about the most fun you're going to have while writing. All that great stuff that's been buzzing around in your head for ages, the giant neon-lit cityscapes, the sleek battle-cruisers, the arid desert planets and the alien trade delegations, all of them can be given life on the page and the only restriction to what they look like and how they work is your imagination. You have all the power now, and no one can stop you!

But Uncle Ben was right, with great power comes great responsibility. You can write whatever you want, but just like effective science, effective world-building requires the right level of detail to make it work visually, and well thought-out, well-connected elements to make sense. Let's look at some of those elements in more detail.

Arguably the two most important world-building elements in any science fiction setting are time and space, but not in the way you're probably thinking. When I say time I don't mean the year in which your story is set — as we've previously mentioned, all science fiction is actually exploring the present day no matter the time period in which it's set. What I mean here is the social/cultural stage that your world is at, and by extension, when I say space I mean the kind of space that your characters inhabit. All of this will be dictated by the relative age of your world, so let's look a bit closer at how this stuff typically works:

First Stage World

At the beginning of the life of your world it will likely be a wilderness of some kind. If there are people, there won't be too many of them and they will likely have very few tools and very little technology. If there are different groups of people, they will likely be distant from each other and rarely interact, any encounter being characterised by distrust. People in

A First Stage World is primitive, nomadic, and filled with hardship.

this world will have plenty of space to themselves, but their dwellings are likely to be small and compact because they lack the tools or technology to build big. As hunter/gatherers there may even be a nomadic side to their behaviour. So dwellings become portable. Although they have plenty of space around them, there may well be inherent danger in spreading out and being alone for any length of time. This could be from the indigenous plants and animals, or from the climate, the weather, or other environmental factors. Religious beliefs, if they exist at all, are likely to be based on the seasons, the planets and stars, fertility, and the fears surrounding birth and death.

Second Stage World

As your world begins to grow into the Second Stage of its life, the first thing we notice is that there are far more people and they have settled into small towns or villages where people know each other and have a sense of community. The dwellings will be permanent and therefore of much more substantial construction, and because there is still plenty of space, they are unlikely to be restricted in size by anything other than technology or practicality. All of these people will need to be fed and this means supplementing the hunting/gathering with farms to grow crops and a means to house and protect them, which in turn will spawn new technologies to help with these issues. At this stage there will also likely be groups of people in different towns and villages spread across larger areas. Despite this geographic spread, it will be safer to travel than it has been because they can travel in numbers and they have knowledge and technology to protect themselves. Also, trade will have started between them, which might mean the invention of money, or it might mean bartering of some kind, or a hybrid of both, and alongside this the idea of the arts and entertainment will be taking hold to amuse people when they are not working. Very likely new religious ideas will have sprung up with different rituals surrounding them and different traditions to be observed. This can lead to a lack of understanding and/or a certain amount of antagonism amongst the differing groups, so the idea of law and of government to protect the population and regulate the smooth running of the community will have taken shape, but this also means the introduction of taxes so that these things can be paid for.

Third Stage World

By the time we reach the Third Stage World, the villages and small towns have grown and there are now lots of people; we are definitely in the time of the city. New technology is everywhere and growing, and because everyone no longer has to contribute to the food supply, there are new commercial enterprises, new factories and shops, new ways to trade far and wide, and new jobs — lots and lots of different jobs. However, the cost of everything has spiralled ever upwards and while people have to earn money to pay for food and shelter, they are likely living in smaller, purpose-built dwellings, with less space around them, eating regulated foods. There will be more and more taxes as the government, military and emergency services, as well as law enforcement needs will have grown hugely and new prosperity will have spawned higher levels of crime. But we now also have the concept of leisure time. People can go shopping for luxury goods, travel is fast, safe, and ubiquitous, as is personal transport, and the arts and entertainment are fully evolved into proper industries. Multicultural societies mean that differences in religious beliefs, traditions, creeds, colours, and so on are widely supported at every level.

Fourth Stage World

The Fourth Stage World is the one that none of us wants to live in — the oppressive, dystopian world of our nightmares. The city now totally surrounds us and very little open land can be seen, if any. The people live in tiny, cramped spaces, which they pay too much for. Advanced technology surrounds them, although not everybody has access to it, and by now unemployment, poverty, and crime are rife because the city cannot sustain the ever-growing population. Taxes are high but government services are poor, inefficient, and corrupt. Leisure time is rarely taken because of the need to earn money and the gulf between rich and poor "Haves" and "Have-nots" is huge. There is little sense of community, people are distrustful of their neighbours, and any idea of religion or belief is fading fast because only "myself" matters.

Fifth Stage World

This is the dying world, the final world stage. The environment has been destroyed, all natural resources are dried up and the air we breathe and the water we drink have been polluted beyond the point of recovery. Food is scarce and disease is everywhere. A small layer of super rich will have insulated themselves from the day-to-day concerns of ordinary people, but eventually there will be nothing left to eat or drink or breathe and humans will die out, leaving a quiet and desolate planet in their wake.

A Fifth Stage World has given itself over to ubiquitous technology. (*Blade Runner*, 1982)

Whether your story takes place on a newly discovered planet or in London of 1830, the relationship that your characters have to the place they live and the tools and technology that surround them will be critical in building your world, but there is one important piece of the puzzle still missing, and here it is: your story will rarely, if ever, sit squarely in one world stage or another. More likely it will take place at some point in-between two of the stages and a good part of it will deal with the effects that going through this giant social and cultural change has on the characters and on their place in this new world stage, as well as the effects on the society at large.

So what social/cultural stage is your world at? More importantly, how can you transcend these archetypes to make them different? Well let's start with the obvious. Choose an early stage world and fill it with new technology. This is a tried and tested formula and can work very well if done right. *Terra Nova* (TV) is set between Stage Five and Stage One by having people from a dying Earth in 2049 cross over to a parallel, prehistoric world to start a new life. However, they have transported new and advanced technologies with them to help with agriculture, health, and education, as well as supply the large military presence that protects the inhabitants from roaming dinosaurs. *Avatar* compares the morality of two worlds by not only bringing new technology to a primitive planet, but by using an incredible new technology to immerse the main character in the environment as one of the indigenous peoples. Finally, Joss Whedon's short-lived but brilliant TV series *Firefly* cleverly melds space travel with a frontier-western sensibility in a between-worlds setting so that the further out from the reaches of The Alliance they are the less technology the people have, or have access to, and the more lawless and frontier-like the planet.

So let's think about your setting. Decide which world stage your story is set in, then grab a piece of paper and ask yourself the 20 basic questions below. The idea is to start laying down an outline, so don't worry about detail. We'll get to that later. Right now I just want you to be sure you know and understand the basic world you're setting your story in. Remember that the answer doesn't have to be one thing or another. A habitable planet is unlikely to consist of one kind of environment, but you could have snowy mountains in the East and rich forest to the North and a single great river that splits the planet in two.

1) What kind of land is the world on? (dry desert, soggy clay, wet marshlands, rocks and gravel, green meadows, oceans)
2) What kind of homes do the people of your world live in? (primitive, portable, basic, advanced, high-tech, large, small)
3) What kind of food do they eat? (natural, home-grown, organic, processed, man-made, all-vegetable, all-animal)
4) How do they get the food? (hunt, gather, grow, buy, barter, state-supplied)
5) What dangers surround them during the day? At night? (plants, wildlife, crime, pollution, environment, disease)
6) Are they safe where they live? (indoors, outdoors, enclosed, open)
7) How do they protect themselves? (hiding or fighting, weapons or guile)
8) What technology is available to the people? (none, primitive, same as now, slightly more advanced, very advanced, like magic)
9) Is it safe/easy to travel? (can they go alone, do they need escorts, are they allowed to travel by the state?)
10) How do they travel? (personal transport, public transport, by air, by water, over land, mechanical or animal)
11) What kind of trade is done? (imported, exported, locally, regionally, what goods, what services)
12) Do they need to work? (yes, no, sometimes, are they rich, poor, disabled)
13) What work do they do? (office/sedentary, outdoor/active, cerebral/physical, skilled/non-skilled)
14) What government exists? (totalitarian/anarchic, dictatorship/democracy, theocracy/plutocracy/democracy)
15) Do they have religion? (state decreed or personal choice, private or open worship, many or one, tolerance between them)
16) How tolerant are the people of different races, religions, creeds, etc. (open and tolerant, non-tolerant and aggressive, ambivalent)

17) How do families live? (together/apart, do the young support the elderly?)
18) How long do people generally live? (naturally/unnaturally, short/long)
19) Is everyone educated? (privately or by the state, freely or with strict guidelines, both sexes equally)
20) In general, is the world a negative world or a positive world? (from who's point of view?)

This is not an exhaustive list by any means, and we can — and will — build on it as we go on, but it will give us a very solid foundation upon which to begin building. At the end of the exercise you should be able to construct a paragraph that describes your world well enough to satisfy most people and will look something like this:

To the north, Corvonia is a lush, green and verdant land developed mostly as pasture for the many types of specially bred livestock. The clay subsoil and the temperate climate makes it easy to grow a variety of crops but a mid-year dry season with scorching winds means that care must be taken with cover and irrigation at these times. The market capital, Corvon, has a standing population of only 4,000 with an additional 1,000 or so attracted every year to the AgriTech College which, despite the exorbitant fees, is always over-subscribed due to its outstanding reputation. The bulk of the population, however, comes from the Garrison Waystation which brings an increase of 12,000 troops every 146 days, a welcome presence that brings huge financial benefits to local traders and deters all possible aggressors despite the fact that it mostly fills the taverns and brothels around the Trans-Port. Trade with the south is open and regular, providing an additional income, but since the hostilities began the cost of transporting goods across the vast lakes that separate the two halves have escalated by around 40% and there are fears that soon it may no longer be economically viable to continue. Government administrators have been asked to intervene to ensure safe transit across open water, but currently the Worshipful Khagawl refuses to recognise Corvonia's neutral status and there are fears they may be drawn into the conflict. Currency is the Corvonian Copec.

A pet peeve

Almost every time you come across an inhabited planet in science fiction it is treated as if it's a desert island in the middle of a vast ocean. There is one race, one nation, one government, one currency, one city, and so on. While there might be good reason for this — for example, it's a small colony — on the whole it's just dumb writing. Just take a look at Earth; many races, many nations, many governments and so on and all different colours and creeds and religions with differing customs, all of them usually either at war with, or allied to, some other nation.

TV is the biggest culprit for this with shows like *Dr. Who*, *Star Trek*, and *Stargate: SG1*. To a certain extent, I get it; they have limited budgets and limited time and they need to introduce planet-of-the-week and get in and get out as soon as possible, but really, it's not an excuse. And if you're writing films, you have no excuse. Give your world richness and depth and believability by giving them diverse inhabitants.

ESTABLISHING RULES

No matter what your setting — and let's face it, the choices are infinite — you will be required to explain yourself at some point. To do this you need to have credible explanations at hand, and so you need to establish some hard and fast rules for your world. You can happily have floating mountains and two moons and any number of other weird and wonderful things, and they will look spectacular, but if you can't explain why they are this way — no matter how ridiculous the explanation — the idea will fail. This isn't because people want to judge you in any way, or because knowing your science is important. It's because people need to be able to relate to your world by comparing it to their own, and having explanations for the things in it helps with that.

You don't need hundreds or thousands of rules. As with character bios, you need just enough to get writing. But basing your world on real things in our own world grounds them in a way that makes them seem authentic, and this means you have to know what you're talking about. In the same way that you should understand human physiology when creating alien creatures, then you should understand other sciences, arts, skills and trades to successfully create your own versions. Here are a few guidelines to help you set the rules for your world.

1) Know what you're talking about.
If you're going to have huge buildings, then you should understand architectural principles so that you get the scale and proportions right. If you're going to invent a language, then you need to know about lexicons, morphology, syntax (more on this later). Systems of law, banking, or commerce from of our world need to be understood to be successfully re-interpreted, and proper military tactics will lend your armies an air of invincibility.

2) Make it as authentic as possible.
There's no substitute for knowing the details. If it helps you to visualise, then draw maps, draw pictures, choose colours and construct mythologies around your world and its inhabitants — whatever it takes to immerse yourself in your world. There's a good chance that none of it will make it into your screenplay intact, but having these things crystal clear in your own mind will make your description and action sequences come alive.

3) Remember the natural laws of physics.
If your people can fly, then they need big enough wings or light enough bodies or immense power to make it happen. If they can swim underwater for days, they need to be able to breathe with gills or hold their breath for a long — but fixed — amount of time, and this will affect lung capacity and chest size and body shape. If there are different climates or environmental extremes, then different life forms will have adapted to live there and they all need food, they all produce waste, and they all reproduce, so make sure you have a way for them to eat, defecate, and have sex.

4) Understand what is constant in your world.
List out the important constants of your world, whether it's the continents, or the religious hierarchy, or the coin denominations, or which classes of spaceship are capable of which kinds of space travel. If you keep these notes at hand when writing, you'll avoid making continuity errors.

5) Be consistent.

It doesn't matter if the physics of your world aren't real as long as they are consistent and you never break your own rules. If time travel needs 1.21 gigawatts of electricity delivered directly into the Flux Capacitor while doing exactly 88mph in 1985, then you'll need exactly the same in 1955.

SKETCHING THE BACKDROP

If you build a house you don't rush out with bricks and mortar and start slapping it together, you start with a blueprint. You tinker with it until you get it right, then you start building, but not all at once. You lay a foundation, then you put up walls and floors and a roof, then you add utilities, and finally you fit and finish. You build a world in the same way by sketching it out first, then laying foundations, then little details, and finally finishing off.

To get started, have a think about the type of world you're after, then pick somewhere that is already a bit like it. If you want a high-tech industrialised world with people living cheek-by-jowl in very over-crowded cities, then I'd start by looking at Japan or parts of China. If you were thinking about a wilderness world with limited technology populated by nomadic peoples, I'd look to Mongolia or parts of Africa.

Once you have the place fixed in your mind, take a look at things like the population numbers and the kind of dwellings they occupy. Buildings are an important part of a world, but if you want something similar to Japan but with a feel like Italy, then you need to transplant one into the other and start to mash them together. Ask yourself why are the buildings this big, or this shape? Heavy snows mean a pointed roof, dry spells mean flat roofs and water butts. Is the city fortified against attack? Does it have a wall or a barracks and a standing army? Why? Is a threat from an opposing race an imminent threat?

Then think about the government. How does it work? Who is in charge? How are they elected? How is opposition treated? Then ask the same questions about religion and ask yourself how is all this policed? How does the law work? It's often interesting to ask what is the worst crime someone can commit and what punishment does it warrant? In a world where food is scarce and rationing is in place, hiding contraband food could be the worst of all crimes, punishable by banishment and, ultimately, starvation.

Finally, think about commerce, travel, and trade. What is this city's place in the world? Is it an outpost away from the capital, or the mecca for all things? What goods do people trade and what do they buy in return? Is travel free and easy, or expensive and difficult and fraught with danger? How do they travel? Is it by train or spacecraft, or on the back of a mule or some other alien creature?

These are the big backdrop pieces to your world and will quickly get you started, so now let's look at filling in some detail.

DRAWING IN THE DETAIL

The details are where your People, Places, and Technology will come to life. If you get them right your descriptions, characters, and action will leap off the page. If you skimp on the details, then things can quickly get confused or seem artificial. Like I've said before, you can dig as deeply into this as you want to go, but I'd advise you to only do as much as is necessary to get writing. If you're not sure that what you're writing sounds right or if it doesn't ring true, go back to the details and flesh them out. The preparation will always get you out of a hole.

Go back to the buildings you described originally. What colour are they? Hot countries tend to use white or very light colours to reflect heat, and cold countries don't tend to bother with painting, they just make sure they're insulated. Do they have gardens? What do they grow? Vegetables would indicate food issues; flowers would indicate leisure time. How are they arranged? Often you'll find that the poor people live low down in the city, in the industrialised areas or near docks or factories while the richer neighbourhoods are further uphill where the air is cleaner and the view is more impressive.

Think about the culture and customs of the people that occupy the place. Are they very family and community oriented? Does religion play a large part in social life? Are they a raucous and joyous people? People tend to act in one of two ways, one that is natural to them and one that isn't. Do you act the same in a bar with friends as you do at your folks' place for Thanksgiving? No, you don't, and neither will your people. But this works in other ways too. A downtrodden people or a slave race will necessarily be quiet and deferential in front of their oppressors, but they may smile and chat with their own kind. A quiet and introspective people are unlikely to wear garishly coloured clothes or jewellery, and if your main character is someone who goes against the grain then you have instant conflict.

Dejah Thoris (Lynn Collins) teaches John Carter (Taylor Kitsch) about Martian culture. (*John Carter*, 2012)

Similarly, do they have music or dance? Are there feast days and sacrifice days? Are they religious in nature and if so, is there one god or many gods? What are the basic tenets of the belief system? (We tend to forget that western storytelling is largely based on a Judeo-Christian belief system of one person who sacrifices themselves to save us all. Storytelling in China or Japan or Africa is not, and so their stories are very different to ours.) And are they great artists, artisans, or craftsmen? Do they have a rich tradition of poetry or songs that is passed from generation to generation? Think about the lore, legends, and myths of your people and how they impact their beliefs. Do they carry lucky totems around with them? What is their equivalent of the crucifix or the Star of David or the Qur'an.

Finally, look at occupations. What is the economy based on? What jobs are needed to drive this economy? High-tech worlds require engineers and software programmers and support staff. A city-born child surrounded by computers and technology is unlikely to be a farmer and vice versa, and if you transplant one into the other, they will struggle to adapt. Big cities are crowded, noisy, scary places where it's easy to remain anonymous. Small towns or villages seem friendlier somehow and people are much more likely to know one another.

Always remember, make it as authentic as possible. Give your characters clothes, jobs, places to live, superstitions and beliefs that make them very definitely "of this world" and you'll reap the rewards.

EXERCISE FIVE

Back to our planet in Exercise Three.

The bad guys were beaten and everyone is safe. The terraforming exercise went brilliantly well, taking only a couple of years instead of the couple of millennia you might normally expect. Although much of the stock of seeds and wildlife the colonists brought with them made it through intact, vast stores of important flora, in particular a lot of food crops, weren't so lucky and the micro-team of biologists on the surface had to improvise DNA splicing and genetic manipulation to create the variety needed for the harvest to succeed.

Factions have sprung up amongst the colonists and a few have broken away. They aren't openly hostile or antagonistic, but given the distance they now are from an Earth-bound government, they want to live their lives on their own terms. With animals and fish to hunt and the land supporting a versatile breed of farmed crops, they take the opportunity to leave, but this breakaway group doesn't have everything they need to thrive. They make tools and adapt technology to suit their purposes and they are semi-nomadic, exploring their new world while they find exactly the right place to settle, but they also don't want to be too far away from the main camp in case of medical or other emergencies.

Despite the extra-terrestrial setting, what I'm describing here are the people from a Fifth Stage World, now finding themselves living somewhere between First Stage and Second Stage worlds.

Now it's your turn. I want to you describe this new planet, in detail, to someone who has never seen it. Tell them about the landscape and the terrain, the plants and trees that have grown, what is benign, what is harmful, and what is downright dangerous; remember much of the flora and fauna are mutations of things we already know, bred for necessity to get some diversity, so how has that manifested itself on the world? Describe the mountains and streams and valleys, the clouds and sky and lakes, and did the planet contain water that has melted into vast seas or frozen into land-like masses?

There's a lot of scope for your imagination to run wild, but don't forget to do some research as well and make sure that it all makes sense — geographically, topographically, geologically and so on. You want to be able to give this piece of work to an expert and have them find no holes in it. A big ask, but that's the difference between good science and bad science.

Chapter Six

Getting the Science Right, Part 1

❦

Indistinguishable from Magic

The late great Arthur C. Clarke famously said, "Any sufficiently advanced technology is indistinguishable from magic" — and it's true. As I write this, the average teenager carries a mobile device around that, in seconds, will provide answers to questions, translate a language, call up a map and give directions, track their friends, take a photo, and — if they're old-fashioned enough — let them speak with anyone, anywhere in the world, anytime. On top of that they can watch TV, play music and games, or pick from thousands of books to read instantly. Only as far back as 1950, this device would have been seen as advanced alien technology. In 1650 you'd have been burned at the stake as a witch.

Now in fantasy writing you can explain away magic by describing it as "mystical forces drawn from the land" or some such. And as long as your magic system is consistent and there's some cause and effect, you're fine. Science fiction, however, demands that you explain yourself, largely because even high school kids have an understanding of basic science, and if they ask "How does that work?" they won't accept "It just does" as an answer. That doesn't mean you can't be vague and, as we've already seen, you can make it up as you go along if you have enough conviction about it, but you do need to have proper answers to some basic questions.

As I've said before, don't get bogged down in research. You don't need an advanced doctorate in quantum physics to write this stuff. You only need to know enough so you can get it on the page. But if you use machinery, then you should know how it works, how it's built, and what fuels it. If you're going to travel at faster-than-light speeds, then you should understand the physics enough so that you can write about it convincingly and not make a fool of yourself.

Having said that, be prepared to be called out by someone at some-time because there will always be that guy in the audience who worked at CERN and now works at NASA and knows more about FTL theory than anyone else on Earth. You can't beat him. Don't try. But for the rest of the average audience, get the basics right and they will follow you.

WHEN THE SCIENCE MATTERS....

The science always matters. Whenever you're depicting a scientific pro-cedure that needs to be explained, then it matters that it makes sense — even if it's totally made up. The science *really* matters when you're depicting present-day activities or things that we know a lot about.

If your story features the Space Shuttle taking off, then you had better know what that take-off procedure is. Even if you compress the timeline to show it happening on one page, if that one minute of screen time features 20 five-second cuts, they'd better be showing the right stages of take-off in the right order. The same is true when some-one describes a scientific principal; don't "think" you know it, make sure you know it, and then double-check with someone who does know it to make sure you didn't misunderstand it.

Also for things like laboratory procedures; we've all experienced lab work, even at school, and we've seen it on TV and in documentaries, so we understand experiments and controls, clean room principles and hazmat suits, so if you're writing anything involving a lab, then get the details and the procedures right. There are any number of science fic-tion films that feature a laboratory scene, but the good ones all have one thing in common — they feel like real laboratories and the people in them dress and act appropriately and take their work very seriously.

One of my favourite laboratory scenes is the one in *Jurassic Park*. I'm very far from being any kind of scientist, and having a glass-walled lab reminds me a little of watching the cooking process in a Krispy Kreme store, but the conversation that Grant, Sattler, and Malcolm have with the scientists as they watch the raptor egg hatch looks, sounds, and feels real to me — at least real enough to sell it, and that's what counts.

Conversely, I remember watching *Star Wars Episode One: The Phantom Menace* when Liam Neeson, as Qui-Gon Jinn, pipes up about midi-chlorians.

John Hammond (Sir Richard Attenborough) explains the science. (*Jurassic Park*, 1993)

"Without the midi-chlorians, life could not exist, and we would have no knowledge of the Force. They continually speak to us, telling us the will of the Force. When you learn to quiet your mind, you'll hear them speaking to you."

Like a lot of people, my immediate reaction was "the midi-what now?" — and not just because it was a ludicrous and unnecessary piece of exposition, but because it contradicted what we had previously been told about "The Force." Originally — and by originally I mean in *Star Wars* (*Episode Four: A New Hope*) — we were told by Obi-Wan Kenobi that The Force was *"...an energy field created by all living things. It surrounds us and penetrates us. It binds the galaxy together... A Jedi can feel The Force flowing through him."* And while it's a bit mystical and slightly ambiguous, it at least makes sense on a conceptual level. The Force is "an energy field created by all living beings" — we can easily understand that.

But now we have "midi-chlorians" and suddenly, instead of The Force being "an energy field created by all living beings," it's the result of a microscopic life form found inside all of us that we can control to... well, to do what?! The slightly mystical has now become science, so how does it work? How does a Jedi "hear them speaking"? Why can't non-Jedi hear them? Or maybe they can but they just decided not to become Jedi — it's a lot of training after all — and how does that help me lift a crashed X-Wing out of a swamp? It's not clear. Adding bad science to the mix has turned a perfectly plausible, albeit non-scientific, explanation into something farcical.

So be careful about your science. If you're going to have a scientific explanation for something in your story — and you should — then make sure it makes sense, even if it's only at a cursory level.

...AND WHEN IT DOESN'T

It's a tricky balancing act, but the science doesn't matter if it's of no importance to what's going on. If in your world space travel is as ubiquitous as going for take-out then none of your characters will ever talk about it or try to explain it, they'll just do it, and it doesn't matter how it works. If, on the other hand, humans rock up on this incredible world of yours and ask "How do your spaceships fly?" — you'll need to provide an answer that, no matter how cursory and vague, makes some kind of sense.

Whatever it is, it's big! (*Contact*, 1997)

I mentioned *Back to the Future* in Chapter One and it remains a great example of cursory and vague explanations of the science, but there are others that demonstrate this just as well. In 1997's *Contact*, extra-terrestrials send a radio signal to Earth and encoded within it are blueprints for building a craft that can carry just one person. After much wrangling Dr. Ellie Arroway (Jodie Foster) gets a chance to travel in it and, long story short, has a short encounter with an alien being. It's a terrific movie and asks a lot of great questions about "us" along the way, but despite the whole space craft/space travel/alien encounter thing, the science is non-existent and ultimately no one cares because thematically the rest of the movie is great.

The key word here is "feasible." Your science has to be feasible. If it isn't real, then either it isn't mentioned at all because it is of no importance to the story whatsoever, or it has to make absolute sense within the parameters of the world you have constructed so that it can feasibly exist.

Let's face it, the average theatre audience is comprised of postmen and lawyers and bookkeepers and teachers and tattoo artists and web developers and, well, just about any profession you can think of, but it's not full to bursting with cutting-edge scientists. The few that do make it to the multiplex to watch your opus are probably going to be taking the entire scientific output of Hollywood with a giant shovelful of salt, and anyway, they're unlikely to turn up on Reddit, exposing you for the scientific charlatan you so obviously are.

And if they do, so what? You're a writer, not a scientist — but hey, on the bright side, you have just been introduced to the perfect research source for your next screenplay!

RIGHT SCIENCE AND LAZY SCIENCE

Despite the fact that you can make things up and still sound convincing, there are still times when a plausible explanation is difficult to come up with or nothing about your idea makes sense any way you look at it. On occasions like these you can either go Right Science or Lazy Science.

Parker Selfridge (Giovanni Ribisi) gets passionate about Unobtanium. (*Avatar*, 2009)

We've spoken about how to make things as authentic as possible and to understand the natural laws to underpin the science of your world, make it "correct" science in as much as that's possible. **Right Science**, on the other hand, is when there's nothing feasible that answers the basic questions and so you need to pluck something out of thin air to explain it. In this case you need to just choose the right branch of science and hang some plausible sounding words off of your explanation so it sticks. If you can find the right words then you're home-free.

The flip side of that is **Lazy Science**. This is where you've got zip, and a good bit of handwaving and head nodding is the only thing saving you from oblivion. *Another Earth* is a good example of this. Literally another Earth turns up in the sky, not just orbiting our sun, but heading towards us. Now quite apart from the whole "two of everything" debate, which I'd maybe buy into as a plot device, the physics of another planet just popping up next to ours are impossible to believe. The effects of its gravity alone on our planet and on our moon would be enough to destroy us, and for me, the whole concept is ridiculous from the get-go. Still, it was a critical success and it worked on dramatic and other levels so I'm not going to dwell on this too much because, frankly, I don't want to encourage it, but lets work through an example.

One of your characters turns to another and asks *"How do you manage interplanetary travel at such incredible speeds?"*

If you we're writing the correct science, you'd reply *"I'm glad you asked, let me start by showing you the means of propulsion that allows us to bring this ship so close to the speed of light."* They would then go on to mention relativistic speed, the effects of time dilation, hyperspace theory, navigating galactic movements and their coordination, structural design and integrity of intergalactic craft, and the Alcubierre drive.

Yeah, I know, it's unlikely, but you get the drift.

If you were just writing the Right Science you might say something like *"Burning the raw imaginatium ore produces vast amounts of energy that can be harnessed to power the jump drives. Once we figured out how to build ships strong enough to withstand the immense forces, navigating was just simple mathmatics."*

See? It's enough of the right kind of science to be plausible and it doesn't duck the question at all. In reality, this is probably the most science you'll ever write, but as long as you're in the right ballpark in terms of the branch of science and the natural laws, you won't go far wrong.

Now let's look at Lazy Science. Here the reply is likely to be *"Our scientists invented the warp drive thousands of years ago and we have travelled the galaxy ever since."*

They completely ducked the question, did a bit of handwaving and moved on. It's not terrible, but it's not good either and it does relegate your film to B-movie status at best.

If you didn't need the question to be asked, then, of course, it should never come up or you could treat it the way I'd treat someone who asked me how a car worked, by saying *"You push this pedal and steer it with this."* And try for a little comedy, because in a world of ubiquitous space travel, how many people would actually know how it all worked and how many would just own spaceships?

DOING THE RESEARCH

For my money, doing the research is one of the easiest parts of writing science fiction. The scientific community spends an enormous amount of time, effort, and money publishing papers and giving talks doing educational work in order to show people what they're up to and, in the UK at least, there are a number of programs such as those run by SCI-FI-LONDON or the University of Manchester that put scientists in a room with writers to exchange ideas and information and look at the best ways to put the science into fiction.

If you don't have one of these days going on you can always contact your local college or university or a nearby lab and ask to speak to someone. Tell them you're doing research for a screenplay and you would like to discuss the topic with them over coffee; they'll probably be only too willing to talk to you. Just be ready to nod politely when he wants to tell you about his own screenplay in return.

The next most obvious place to find stuff out is the Internet. Google is your friend here, as is Wikipedia, although always double-check the sources. But honestly, you can't throw a stick online without hitting some geeky science website or another, and there's a wealth of fantastic information and a bunch of smart people you can go to for help.

For those of you who need a day trip and like getting out, the public library is your first port of call. Hit the science section and then cross-reference with academic papers and science journals for the latest thinking. Also, make sure you make friends with your librarian, they're an invaluable resource and when they take off those glasses and let their hair down... phew!

Buy some books as well, military histories, biographies, books on economic theory, travel guides; they're all useful to have on hand and you don't need to read them in one go, you can dip in and out of them as you feel like it. One of my favourites is the *New York Public Library Science Desk Reference* that I picked up for a dollar on eBay. Anytime you want to know the diameter of the moon (2,160 miles) or what tachyons are (hypothetical particles that move faster than the speed of light), then it's your go-to book. Another great reference book is *Science Fact and Science Fiction: An Encyclopedia* by Brian Stableford, which is a fabulous source of education in all the ways that science and fiction connect, where science informs the fiction and the fiction inspires the science, covering every conceivable topic from, quite literally, acoustics to zoology.

You should also be regularly watching TV channels like Discovery and History and Wildlife and so on, because they're way better than *America's Got Talent*, you never know what you'll learn, and, more importantly, you never know when it'll come in handy.

EXERCISE SIX

⤜⥈

This is simple enough. Think back to our imaginary planet of previous exercises and describe the terraforming process that made it habitable. I described one method in exercise three but it is only one of a few methods that scientists have speculated upon when thinking about terraforming planets. You'll probably find that the Internet is your friend here and a few minutes of typing into your favourite search engine will yield plenty of results that can be used as the basis for your method, but extrapolate things out, add stuff and take stuff away, speed things up and slow things down, and make the process your own. Above all, make it plausible.

Extra Credit

Describe the terraforming process as action in a screenplay. As you write, imagine that you are watching both from above the planet, looking down, and while standing on the surface, looking out across the landscape as the effects take shape. Make sure to invoke all five senses in your writing to hook us in, don't rely just on the visual spectacle. Describing a smell or a taste or how something feels on your skin is often much more emotive for the reader and a great way of making them really feel what it is you're trying to describe.

CHAPTER SEVEN

GETTING THE SCIENCE RIGHT, PART 2

PLACES

Places exist where it makes sense for them to exist. Cities don't just spring up out of the ground, they start as hamlets, expand to become small villages, grow into big villages which grow into small towns, which become big towns, and along the way they expand outwards and upwards, moving the borders ever further until they meet other big towns coming the other way, and they merge, eventually becoming a big city. But growth is organic, it only occurs when it's necessary, so let's explore some of the things that make that growth necessary, and inevitable.

Being first helps. The first village to be built, named, and occupied will be the one everyone knows and the one they gravitate towards. This isn't always the case, the oldest recorded town in the UK and its first capital was Colchester, in Essex, and it remained that way throughout the early Roman occupation until it was destroyed by Queen Boadicea and London took over the mantle. But it's a lot more than just being first.

To start, we need agriculture. Hunter-gatherers were nomadic peoples, moving as the herds they hunted moved. When people started farming, it encouraged the hunter-gatherers to stop moving and put down roots to be close to a regular food source. They also started to farm animals that they traditionally hunted, so now they had meat to go with their vegetable crops. All this has to be protected from marauders, so a wall is put up around the village, and being a sanctuary increases the population. Inside the walls we find a church, for meetings and for prayer, and probably an inn. This is the start of a decent-sized village.

Of course areas where farming was very successful had a surplus. At first, farmers who grew different crops would barter and trade with one another. Over time this became a regular weekly or monthly event, and suddenly our village has a market day. Market day starts to attract people from outside the village, they come with their own stuff to trade, and this influx of people brings with it other needs. They want somewhere to stay, and they need to eat and drink, so more inns spring up and maybe some stables. Eventually some of the market stalls become permanent establishments and the first shops arrive — the tailors, milliners, haberdashers — and the service industries grow as well — the blacksmiths, coopers, carpenters and so on, and the village everyone travels to on market day becomes a market town.

A wretched hive of scum and villainy. (*Star Wars*, 1977)

This change in status almost inevitably means crime. Most likely a brothel to start, but then gambling and drugs, which lead to debt and turf wars, which means fighting and the occasional death. The town then has to establish proper law enforcement. A police force is formed and law courts and a prison are built. Prisoners need work, so a manufacturing base is formed around cheap labour. The town's legal function grows to become a hub for administrative duties, and all this needs paying for, so taxes are levied and a whole new population layer of lawyers and clerks and bankers join the wealthy merchant classes. This means more opportunities for employment, bigger incomes, better education, and suddenly the market town has become a big town. Farmers have to grow crops at a large enough scale to support the much bigger population, which means industrialisation. Everything becomes more complex; housing, utilities, sanitation, healthcare, emergency services, taxation — all interdependent, all providing opportunities for business. Suburban areas are created on the outskirts for people to live. Offices and factories are built and the suburbanites commute to work. Our big town is now a small city.

Finally, I should talk about logistics. Big cities need a means of exporting and importing stuff. They cannot be sustained unless they are connected to the outside world in some way. If they don't, then they wither and die, which means rioting, unrest, and revolution. Think about how your city is connected to the rest of the world. How do people communicate? How do people travel? How long does it take? Is it dangerous? And so on.

I don't want to spend too much more time on this except to say remember all this when you describe your places. Cities are complex and they don't exist unless there is an infrastructure to support them. Don't describe your city as being surrounded by barren, decaying wastelands unless all the people are starving and dying inside for lack of food. And if you do, have some credible way of providing for the people at least.

PEOPLE

Just like places, people need to be of the place they are from. Skin, eye, and hair colour evolves in direct relation to sun exposure and diet. People from hot sunny climates tend to be darker skinned than those from cooler climates. Taller people are better for seeing at distance over long grasses, and they can also pick fruit more easily. Leaner, longer musculature is better suited to short bursts of explosive power, while shorter, thicker musculature provides better stamina. Shorter people move more quickly and generally have better balance, and on uneven terrain, evolve larger feet and hands.

The epicanthal fold we see in the eyes of Asian races helps in dealing with cold, while rounder western eyes dissipate heat more efficiently. Larger and more sensitive noses are needed where sense of smell is imperative to survival, wider and more narrow noses deal better with heat and cold respectively. At high altitude, barrel-shaped chests with large cavities perform better, while the opposite is true for water-dependant races where swimming is valued. In women, larger breasts promise better milk production.

All of these things are the basic science of people and how they evolve to suit the place they're from. When describing races of people, make sure they have the sound and physical details suited to their home environment. Make sure strangers stand out as such by describing how they are different to the natives, and enhance that by choosing an occupation that suits their natural development.

About Robots

Robot stories are about personal identity and what it means to be human, usually by exploring issues of free will, volition, empathy, and compassion. These issues are at the very heart of the current zeitgeist as we worry about the impersonal nature of our tech-connected lives, about giant, nameless and faceless corporations destroying the economy and ruining lives, about losing our unique personalities in favour of a collection of online personae, and also with the increase in identity theft and the feeling of powerlessness that permeates modern society. Robots are the man-made personification of all of those worries. We bask in our own brilliance as we create these new technologies and then throw up our hands in despair when we lose our jobs to a machine that doesn't get sick, take breaks, or need vacation time or wages.

The counter to robotic behaviour are the things I just mentioned, the ability to empathise, to recognise the feelings and the experiences of others and, in seeing their suffering, to respond with compassion, one of the cornerstones of humanity. This ability goes hand-in-hand with having the free will and volition to respond in this way.

I'm sure you are familiar with Isaac Asimov's Three Laws of Robotics:

1) A robot may not injure a human being, or, through inaction, allow a human being to come to harm.

2) A robot must obey the orders given to it by human beings, except where such orders would conflict with the First Law.

3) A robot must protect its own existence as long as such protection does not conflict with the First or Second Laws.

These three laws pre-suppose that robots have no free will and
cannot act under their own volition. They are specifically designed to
remove from a robot any notion of empathy or compassion. A robot,
in following these laws, is analysing a given situation as a set of data
points that can be evaluated and compared to a simple set of criteria,
and acting according to the strict letter of the law.

Andrew Martin (Robin Williams) is growing on Little Miss (Embeth Davidtz).
(*Bicentennial Man*, 1999)

Several films have tried to humanise robots by giving them the
ability to empathise. In 2001's *A.I. Artificial Intelligence*, a robot boy,
David, is built that feels undying love toward his mother, but when
her real son, who has been in cryostasis awaiting a cure for a disease,
returns home, David is put out of the house to fend for himself.
Wanting nothing more than to return to his mother, David sets off to
find the blue fairy so he can become a real boy and win back her love.

In *Bicentennial Man*, based on the Asimov short story, Andrew Martin is an android programmed to perform household chores. Within days he shows abilities way beyond that of a normal robot, exhibiting emotions and articulating them precisely. Over a period of 200 years, Andrew first learns and absorbs the intricacies of being human, and eventually fights for the legal right to become a man with the ability to die.

So can we find new ways of looking at robots? It's easy to see the many ways that robots being put to work in situations where it would be dangerous for humans — such as in space, underground, or deep underwater — but what about in daily life? Can we really use robots as police, or doctors, or lawyers if they can only enact the letter of the law, without empathy? How can these situations lead to new and unique dramatic conflict?

If a robot does develop free will and acts of its own volition, then does it cease to be owned? And if it commits a crime, who is responsible? Would there be a bedding-in period where the robot is still learning the ropes, as it were, and becomes confused about right and wrong? And what if it creates great art or becomes a successful business owner? How does it benefit from income and does it have to pay taxes?

Robots can act as stand-ins for all kinds of reasons, but always remember, in the end your story is always going to be about what it's like to be human.

TRAVELLING THROUGH SPACE

While we'd like to have wormholes, tractor beams, artificial gravity, FTL travel, jump drive engines, etc., we can't. In fact, we can only use the physics we have, NOT the physics we want.

It goes without saying that a lot of science fiction takes place in space, whether it's on space stations, space craft, or in space colonies where humans live on distant planets. Over the years, as fans have become more aware of the trials and tribulations of space travel, the need to heed those issues in its depiction has grown. Now the usual way to do this is to claim that the planet is "Earth like" and that we can all live and breathe and walk and go about our daily lives exactly as if we were back home, but that doesn't really cut it with the informed sci-fi audience.

As with all things science fiction, this doesn't mean you have to abandon your story because the effects of space travel on the human body render your plot unlikely or ridiculous, but it does mean that the solutions to these effects and the problems they cause have to be feasible, preferably making use of Right Science to lend the proper authenticity to your scenes. A round trip to Mars using current technology is estimated to involve at least two years of travelling time with a wait of a few months on the planet itself between journeys. Humans have not stayed for that long in space before. At present, 188 days is the longest any human has remained in space. Stays of this length have resulted in very severe medical problems for astronauts returning to Earth, so let's briefly look at some of them.

The crew of the Antares prepare to start walking. (*Defying Gravity*, 2009)

Cardiovascular System

We know that one of the biggest forces affecting us on Earth is gravity, and we know that humans are made up of an enormous amount of fluids. Gravity would ordinarily force these fluids to pool in the lower body as we sit or stand, but our bodies have a lot of pumps and valves and other mechanisms that prevent this from happening and keep blood flowing to the brain. Without gravity, an effect known as "fluid shift" sees these fluids flow freely around our bodies however they see fit, causing nasal congestion and leaving us with stuffy noses, puffy faces and headaches as if we have a permanent cold. The systems our bodies have for controlling blood pressure also suffer as they are no longer in use and the return to Earth usually means problems with standing for any period, although our bodies always recover over time.

Balance & Motion Sickness

Because of the effects of gravity on Earth our bodies constantly seek to re-adjust to prevent us from falling over. In space, the lack of gravity has a huge effect on our inner ear, our eyes, and on our systems of balance, such as the contraction of muscles in our legs and feet, so we very quickly have trouble orienting ourselves to decide which way is up. This trouble with orienting ourselves due to weightlessness causes space motion sickness in 60-70% of all astronauts and is characterised by headaches, nausea, vomiting, and a general malaise.

Bones & Muscles

We all know that the human skeleton is there to hold our bodies upright and that the bones are made up of calcium and phosphorous. Prolonged weightlessness leads to the severe depletion of both calcium and phosphorous in our urine, which leads to greatly reduced bone density. In tests of astronauts on the ISS, around 3% per month. All the time someone is in space this isn't an issue, but once back on Earth or anywhere with full gravity it could lead to problems standing or walking and even breaks or fractures due to the weakening of the bone structure as well as problems with breathing and respiration. It is still not yet known whether bones recover fully over time upon our return. Weightlessness will also lead to the atrophying or wastage of muscle because the forces needed to propel ourselves or to lift or carry things are so small that we cease using them.

Radiation

On Earth we are shielded from radiation from space by our atmosphere and by a natural magnetic shielding. Outside of our atmosphere this shielding doesn't exist and thus astronauts are subject to much greater doses of radiation than the rest of us, resulting in decreased immune system function and increased risk of disease spreading around crews, but also for cancers, cataracts, and blood diseases.

Food
Foods appear to have little taste, feeling bland. Foods we don't normally eat can become palatable. This could be the effects of fluid shift on our faces or of radiation on stored foods, or even boredom due to restricted diet.

Sleep
Variable cycles of light and dark along with poor illumination during daytime hours can have very negative effects on the quantity and quality of sleep. Just like the rest of us, this upset in circadian rhythms can aggravate any psychological stresses astronauts are already experiencing.

Dr. Holly Goodhead (Lois Chiles) and James Bond (Roger Moore) adjust remarkably quickly to space travel. (*Moonraker*, 1979)

Psychological Effects
The enormous stress of performing complex duties, coupled with the physical effects on the body, environmental changes and interpersonal issues arising from such close proximity to a small number of crew, will inevitably lead to psychological issues. It has been observed that there are three distinct phases of psychology in space. Phase One, the first

couple of months, people are busy adapting to the new environment and remain upbeat. Phase Two sees distinct signs of fatigue and crews become de-motivated. Phase Three astronauts exhibit signs of hypersensitivity and they become nervous and irritable. There's no cure, but lighter work and frequent communication with family do a lot to boost morale.

These issues are important but treatable on the short space flights we have at the moment, and even on slightly longer-term stays such as those on the ISS, but imagine the effects they would have on space colonisation. The amount of medical equipment and the ability to treat symptoms would be paramount in the success of any truly long-term endeavour to settle or colonise a distant planet.

A lot to think about, isn't it? But now let's look at logistics. As the late, great Douglas Adams told us, "Space is big. No, really big." So with this in mind, let's think a little about the logistics of travelling in space, and I warn you the numbers are big. No, really big.

Escape Velocity
To get a rocket to leave the Earth it needs to reach "escape velocity," which is 11.2km/s or 7mps or 25,200mph or Mach34 (34x the speed of sound). But escape velocity is not a constant. It decreases as you increase your altitude, and as well as gravity. It is affected by wind resistance, weather, direction in relation to rotation of the Earth, distance from the Equator, and probably a bunch of other things I'll never know or understand. But I do understand that escape velocity on Earth will be different than from the Moon, or Jupiter, or Pluto.

Distances
Distances in space are very often quoted in light years, that is the time it takes for a beam of light to travel between two points, approximately 300,000km/s or 186,000 mps. That's blazingly fast. If we could ever hit those speeds, then the Moon, which takes a manned space flight around 3 days to get to, could be reached in only 1.3 light-seconds!

Supplies
So what kinds of supplies would an average space crew need to take with them when heading off to boldly go, etc. Well according to the

MIT Space Logistics Centre, the classes of supplies identified include:

- Propellants and Fuels
- Crew Provisions and Operations
- Maintenance and Upkeep
- Stowage and Restraint
- Waste and Disposal
- Habitation and Infrastructure
- Transportation and Carriers
- Miscellaneous

See, people know this stuff. I'm sure if you asked nicely they'd sit down with a cup of coffee and explain it to you.

Artificial Gravity
Centrifugal force is a balance between momentum and gravity. The physics are simple, but actually, artificial gravity is hard to do. Centrifugal force is often depicted as a way of providing some kind of gravity. We should remember that the gravity is always zero at the centre of the spiral. If we launched smaller ships, then we'd need to take advantage of what's available. *Babylon 5* launched its fighters by turning them outwards and dropping them. They'd turn on power once they were away.

There is a rich tradition of stories set purely in space that ask the really big questions about religion, about the existence of or belief in a higher being, about the purpose of life, the inevitability of death and what might lie beyond. They question, at their heart, what it's like to be us, to be human, what our place in the universe might be and whether we really are ready to start exploring the stars.

The big problem with movies like this is the grand list of overused science fiction clichés that will inevitably crop up. I've lost count of how many times I've seen a crew awakening from cryostasis sleep or a ship designed with an AI computer controlling everything and at the end to find a huge mega-corporation or government military project is behind the funding. All the staples of space travel — the spacesuit, the spacewalk, the cosmic storm, the lunar RV — have all been done to death, but it will take a smart mind to cook up something different with such a limited number of ingredients.

THE PHYSICS OF SPACE

Lasers

First things first, you can't normally see a laser beam, you can only see where the beam has touched something, and if you can see the beam, what you are actually seeing is scattered light being reflected off of particles in the air and any light you actually see is no longer laser light.

With enough power you could probably use a laser to slice through sheet metal in space the same way as we use them here on Earth, and because in space a laser beam would travel in a straight line pretty much forever we could probably do it at some distance. The problem with this plan, though, is that the chances of being able to generate the kind of power necessary to achieve this are pretty remote. That said, everyone knows that you never look directly into a laser beam (you do know that, don't you?) so we could probably use small lasers to blind our enemy, or at least blind his cameras and monitors. Beyond that I don't hold out much hope for lasers in space.

What we can see are either radio waves or microwaves and they vary in strength:

- Red = weak
- Green = better
- Blue = much better
- Purple = best

But the best source for weapons would be x-rays or gamma rays and, unfortunately for Hollywood, they're totally silent and completely invisible.

One way of making this work would be a particle beam. It has mass so you can see it, it has energy so you can feel it, it comes in any colour you like and it's much more powerful than any laser. Try to imagine, a bullet travels at 200m/sec, a shell travels 1500m/sec. A particle beam travels at 99.995% of the speed of light (186,000 miles per second) that's more than 300,000,000 meters per second.

Momentum

Basic physics can be traced from man's earliest weapons to its newest. If you remember your basic physics, you'll know that an object in motion shall remain in motion (until acted upon by an outside force). With this in mind, the most bang-for-buck effective weapon you could have in space would actually be kinetic energy, or "throwing stuff" to you and me. It's crude, and not very sexy, but mass is much more effective than lasers and still hurts when it hits. In fact, the only dependency for its effectiveness is velocity, or how hard and fast you can actually throw the projectile.

This is also true for multiple projectiles, so if something breaks up while in motion in space, then each of the pieces will be travelling at the same speed when they hit a target. With no atmosphere, no gravity, and no friction in space, chucking a rock, if you can throw it hard enough, can be just as devastating as any weapon you can imagine, and survival in space is so hard anyway that just disabling your enemy would be enough to keep them busy while you slipped away.

Cloaking

We already have a kind of cloaking, in "stealth" technology that confuses radar. Now cloaking as "invisibility" means that light goes right through an object, but the trouble with invisibility is that the things that you touch, or traces you leave, find you out.

If light bends around an object it can render it invisible, but the power required to make it happen is huge. It also creates a duplicate image where the light re-converges, although this could be used to confuse.

And what about the light and heat that you emit? It needs to be diffused in some way or else there will be visible distortion effects.

Oh, and if you bend light away from your field of vision you won't be able to see either. So that's an issue.

Light is made up of photons that are just about the fastest things ever. Light travels at 3×10^8 m/sec ($E=\frac{1}{2}mv^2$) and light from the sun still takes 8 minutes to get here. Trekkers will know that this gives rise to the "Picard Manoeuvre" — gaining 10 seconds of invisibility from a warp jump to a point in space (or as long as it takes for the light to get from one ship to the other) is enough time to open fire and then jump away again.

Explosions

The power of an explosion in space actually comes from the pressurised air inside of a space craft and the lack of air pressure in space. Air on Earth = 15 lbs per inch^2 but we don't notice because we're born here and we've evolved to cope. But in space, 15 lbs per inch^2 is huge, so if a hull breached we'd get "explosive decompression" as the pressurised air exploded out into space, taking everything with it.

Sound

Energy cannot be created, it can only change form. Sound is created by compressed waves of air. It needs air in order to travel from ear to ear. No air in space means no way to have longitudinal waves travel, which means NO SOUND! Now I know that this is cinema and using sound for explosions in space is "cinematic," though Joss Whedon's brilliant but short-lived series *Firefly* always portrayed space as totally silent and they used that silence, and the waiting for something to make a sound, to develop tension. Try to use the inherent tension of enforced silence to your advantage in your screenplays rather than pretend sound exists in space.

A WORD ABOUT TIME TRAVEL

Ever since H.G. Wells published *The Time Machine*, the idea of being able to travel either backwards or forwards in time has fascinated humans. Doubtless many far cleverer people than I could tell you why, but my theory is that it's to do with the idea of second chances, that somehow things would be better if we could only escape the confines of this time and move on, or else go back and put right the things we left undone. Inevitably, though, things are not that simple.

In science fiction films time travel takes two basic shapes:

1) A character travels through time.
2) A character meets someone who has travelled through time.

In the first case the driving force of the story can simply be to get the character back home, but often they have gone specifically to perform some task. Going back in time is usually about changing something in the past to make the present different or better in some way, while travelling to the future is about returning to the present armed with

116

Mr. Wells (Rod Taylor) looks forward to his journey. (*The Time Machine*, 1960)

knowledge that will benefit in some way. In the second case our main character meets or is visited by a traveller from either the past or the future and the driving force is to find a way of getting them back to their own time. When the traveller is from the future, there is often a warning of some kind to be imparted.

In either of these cases the same basic issues of cause and effect need to be carefully addressed to make the story work. First there is the problem of tampering with events. In the first instance there are the unknowables; for example, could stepping on a beetle in the distant past cause some profound change in the present? Then there are the knowables, like if you knew the lottery numbers in advance should you take advantage for selfish reasons? Thirdly there are the paradoxes, the most famous being the Grandfather Paradox. In this instance a traveller goes back in time and kills his grandfather at a time before his grandfather met his grandmother. This means that either his mother, or his father, would not have been born and thus neither would the time traveller himself so he could not have gone back in time to kill his grandfather. (Yikes!)

The expression "Butterfly Effect" comes from a 1952 Ray Bradbury short story called *A Sound of Thunder*, made into a film of the
same name in 2005. In it a hunter by the name of Eckels pays to go
back in time from 2055 so he can hunt a T-Rex. The guides stress the
importance of not changing anything and only killing animals that
were going to die within minutes anyway (this particular T-Rex was
due to be hit by a falling tree), but come the time, Eckels loses his
nerve and steps off the path. The guides kill the T-Rex, but when they
get home their world has changed in subtle ways and later, when he
looks at his boots, Eckels discovers a butterfly crushed into the mud on
the soles.

This "time safari" is about to cause mankind a huge headache. (*A Sound of Thunder*, 2005)

A lot of Alternate History/Alternate Reality stories have a basis
in time travel, the proviso being that somewhere along the timeline
there was some kind of cosmic "decision point" where every choice was
made, every decision acted upon, resulting in every possible outcome,
each one existing separately, nestled in a parallel universe to our own.
The inference is that:

a) The smallest decision by anyone can change the course of an entire world.
b) There is no such thing as fate or destiny, our lives are our own and we control them. (This is, of course, completely paradoxical if you believe "a").

These types of stories can be either negative or positive. *Minority Report* suggests that despite everything we try, our path is fixed and our destiny is set, we have no free will. The pre-cog system is never wrong, the future is certain and cannot be changed. Conversely, in *Timecop*, Walker (Jean-Claude Van Damme) is part of a police unit called TEC that ensures no crimes are committed by changing things in the past. This is particularly abhorrent for Walker as his wife was murdered the day he joined the unit, but the story suggests that we can change our lives and our destiny if only we could change the past, and this sets up the ending of the film.

In both *Donnie Darko* and in *The Butterfly Effect*, the protagonists realise that the only way to change things for the better is to remove themselves from the world, to sacrifice themselves for the good of others. In *Donnie Darko*, Donnie, while sleepwalking, narrowly escapes death when the engine from a passenger jet crashes into his bedroom. Simultaneously, a vision tells him the world will end in 28 days, so 28 days later, when Donnie's new girlfriend is killed in a traffic accident, he knows that the only way to change things is to go back in time and be killed by the jet engine.

In *The Butterfly Effect*, Evan (Ashton Kutcher) has stress-blackouts where he wakes up somewhere else with no recollection of events. Eventually he figures out that he can time-travel back to these traumatic events and change things to make his life better, but the consequences of his time-travelling are always bad for someone else and he cannot fix things to be perfect for everybody. In the end he goes back to the most important moment for him, changes that, and then destroys his path back so that events play out for people as they should, without his interference.

It's almost always these kinds of paradoxes that undo time travel stories no matter how well they have been constructed. If that happens, you have two choices. Either a) be prepared to spend a lot of time working through your story and pulling your hair out as you try to resolve your paradox, or b) shrug your shoulders and work on making the story really entertaining so the paradox doesn't matter.

EXERCISE SEVEN

I want you to change time. I mean everyone knows it's a given that if you can ever go back in time you have to kill Hitler, but as a choice that's a bit too easy and besides WW2 has been used enough. See *Fatherland, It Happened Here*, or for a bit of fun, try the UK TV show *Misfits* (Series 3, Episode 4), where an elderly Jew travels back in time to kill Hitler but fails, and the Nazis reverse-engineer the technology from his mobile phone to win the war.

What I want you to do is take a historical world event and try three exercises:

1) Imagine it didn't happen.
2) Imagine it happened differently.
3) Imagine it happened the same way but the outcome was different.

Write out what the consequences might be. Ask yourself:

1) Who benefited and who lost out?
2) Who lived and who died?
3) How were politics changed?
4) How did the economy change?
5) How was technology changed?
6) Did it affect civil rights?
7) Did it affect civil liberties?
8) Did it have any effect on the arts? (Literature, painting, music, etc.)
9) Has culture (language, traditions, religion) changed as a result?
10) How has it affected international relations?

Answering these questions will give you the basis of a good science fiction story; why not take the opportunity to flesh the ideas out with the exercises in Chapter Two.

Extra Credit
Think of a famous person who died young (JFK, Jimi Hendrix, Marilyn Monroe, Martin Luther King, etc.) and write what might have happened if they'd lived. What would have changed? What would they have accomplished? How might things be different for the rest of us? And importantly, if they were still alive, what would they be doing now?

Chapter Eight

"George, you can type this shit, but you sure as hell can't say it."

The Dialogue of The Future

If convincing dialogue is one of the hardest things to get right for anyone writing a screenplay, convincing dialogue for a science fiction film is probably even harder. In a genre where conversations routinely make passing reference to hyperspace, AI networks, and plasma rifles, it can be hard sometimes not to stifle a giggle when the dialogue moves from the seemingly everyday to the patently ludicrous.

The Emperor (Christopher Plummer) can't believe it's come to this. (*Starcrash*, 1978)

There are many famous examples of silly science fiction dialogue, but more than a few of the all-time greats come from Roger Corman's 1978 *Star Wars* rip-off *Starcrash*, in which Christopher Plummer, faced with certain death, utters the immortal line "*Imperial Battleship, halt the flow of time!*" — a level of equipment that I've not seen on a space craft before or since. The same film also features a young David Hasselhoff in the midst of the climactic battle scene yelling "*Fourth-dimensional attack!*" — which I'm still scratching my head at even now.

The fact is that if you're not careful, science fiction paves the way for the worst kind of dialogue excess, and while that may be an opportunity for humour, most often belly-laughs are not the intended reaction, and so, as with all science fiction writing, we have to apply some thought to what people say.

THE WAY PEOPLE SPEAK

First of all, let's have a look at the way people speak. Now I'm not even going to try and write a full discourse on writing movie dialogue — for that you should check out Penny Penniston's excellent book *Talk The Talk* — but I do want to point out a couple of common mistakes and explore some good principles.

A lot of screenplays that I read have dialogue that reads a bit like this:

```
                TERRY
    Hi Bob, you look terrible,
    like you haven't slept.


                BOB
    Oh hey Terry, well I didn't
    get much sleep last night.
    Workmen turned up around 2am
    and started digging the road up
    right outside my apartment.
    I asked them what was going
    on and they said it was a leaking
    gas main that needed emergency
```

```
repair work. In the end I had to
spend £40 on a cheap motel room
and still only got 3 hours sleep.
```

It may give you all the information you need, but straight away you'll notice it's too formal and doesn't sound natural, because in reality people actually talk like this:

```
              TERRY
'Sup man, look like shit.


              BOB
Yeah, no... oh man...
bastards... started like,
ummm digging the road up
at like, I dunno, like
two or somethin'? Erm
fuckin' gas emergency...
wow... noise man, like
braaaaargh! Fuck. Had umm,
had to get outta there.
Sprung like, forty quid on
some fleapit and still only
got like 3 hours kip.
```

The differences are obvious. Real people tend towards much more informal speech patterns with hesitation in the shape of *umm*'s and *err*'s and disjointed sentences. Between male friends especially, speech is often peppered with casual profanity but it also contains slang expressions such as *quid* instead of *pounds*, *fleapit* instead *motel*, *kip* instead of *sleep*. In the first example you'll also notice that the two characters call each other by name, whereas in reality we rarely, if ever, mention the name of the person we're talking to. You know who you're speaking to and they know you're talking to them, so it would feel weird.

Another aspect of real speech is that we tend to emphasise our own side of any story, so in this case Bob is portraying himself as the victim, as if the whole incident were a deliberate ploy to ruin his night. We also like to imitate the dramatic stuff, act it out for greater effect, so we get "... *noise man, like braaaaargh!*" to demonstrate how loud the digging was.

Hopefully you'll agree that the second example is much better than the first — it has life, it has personality, and it has colour — but it's also overlong. We're not writing a novel, and speech patterns like this will add 20 or 30 pages to your script, so clearly we need to find some middle ground. The easiest way to start is by tidying up the speech, get rid of the *umm*'s and *err*'s, remove the superfluous "like" adverbs, don't drop last letters, and remove the profanity.

The end result might look something like this:

```
          TERRY
What's up man, you look bad.


          BOB
They started digging my road
up at two, gas emergency, had
to go to a motel. Forty quid
for three hours sleep.
```

I think this is a nice balance between formal enough to be easily understood, and casual enough, with just enough slang, to sound natural. It's also much shorter. We have all the information we need from this exchange without adding significantly to the page count.

Of course, when trimming dialogue like this you have to be careful that you don't end up with all of your characters sounding the same. Not being able to tell who is speaking is a common problem in a lot of screenplays, but there are a few tricks to overcome this.

One thing to try is assigning a descriptive word or two to a character, something that becomes a part of their everyday speech patterns and singles them out whenever you hear it. In my screenplay *Outpost One*, "Rocket" Ronnie Bray says "splendid" all the time. He also refers to everyone as either "Young man" or "Young lady," ostensibly because he's the oldest member of the crew, but actually it's because he's terrible with names.

You can use the same trick with things that people refuse to say. An easy way to do this is to have one person who absolutely never swears or cusses, especially if their upbringing or background has a religious or social imperative that frowns on profanity. I used this trick with a character in a group that absolutely refused to acknowledge someone by rank.

Throughout the screenplay they never once called her Captain, Cap'n, or Skipper, like the rest of the crew. They only referred to her by name.

If you make a character a native speaker of a foreign language, German for example, then don't fake it by having them *"Haf vays of making you talk."* When people speak foreign languages, with very few exceptions, they don't slip in and out of English, as they are concentrating on the right words. They may stumble or they may have problems with accent, but the words will be English. If you want to remind the reader that this character is German, then very occasionally have them finish a sentence and then mutter under their breath in German or, if there's another German speaker in the scene, have them confer with them in their native language. Both would be much more natural ways to express themselves.

Most importantly, don't forget that people like to joke, flirt, make excuses, argue, interrogate each other, tease each other, teach each other, compliment each other, tell secrets, tell lies, try to seduce, and sometimes, very occasionally, they just sit there and don't say anything at all.

By far the best method for getting dialogue right is to record real conversations and then listen to them back, transcribing them word for word. Joe Cornish, writer/director of the fabulous *Attack the Block*, went to a youth club and recorded conversations he had with groups of kids there in order to nail the street slang that his characters used in the film. But to keep the audience from getting confused, he isolated six or seven key words and phrases that kept coming up and he restricted the dialogue in the film to those key phrases. Because of this, even if you don't know the patois that these kids use, it doesn't take very long watching the film to be able to understand everything they're saying.

If you don't have that luxury, then try recording a chat show, or better yet a political debate on TV. Without the benefit of facial expressions, hand gestures or body language, it's astounding how incoherent and rambling is the gibberish that supposedly educated people spout when you just isolate the words. You'll also find that people — and personally I'm terrible for this — use clichés all the time when they speak and this can fool you into thinking your dialogue sounds natural. Unless it's a character trait you've deliberately decided upon, don't do it. Find a nice, simple active sentence to say instead; your audience will thank you for it.

It's Pest, Moses, Jerome, Biggz, and Dennis innit. (*Attack the Block*, 2011)

The last thing I'll mention here is that the best way to test your dialogue is always to read it out loud. It works, and better yet, if you can organise a few people to do a "table reading" for you of just your dialogue while you sit and listen, you'll really find out if it's working. Because when you hear it out loud, if it sounds forced or unnatural in any way, then it probably needs a re-write.

MAKE IT MAKE SENSE

There will always be jargon associated with science fiction films. It's inherent in the genre. Anytime you discuss new technology or scientific principles, complex processes or advanced systems, it is inevitable that those who know them and operate them will develop a shorthand based on acronyms and technical terms mixed-in with pop-culture references and slang that only they will understand. This knowledge will often surface a kind of inverted snobbery, especially between people who "do" and management who "don't" because as the old saying goes, in the kingdom of the blind, the one-eyed man is king.

What we as writers of science fiction must be careful of is the use of baffling, nonsensical faux-technology, pompous and ludicrous-sounding names for things, and inaccurate use of real scientific terminology — the world's worst offender being *Star Trek*. Actors on the show have freely admitted that they often just "*made up words that sounded technical*" and "Treknobabble," as it became known, was such a huge source of comic relief for audiences (despite not actually meaning to be) that eventually the writers started to parody their own shows with it, with Q from *Star Trek: Deep Space 9* given the line "*Picard and his lackeys would have solved all this technobabble hours ago.*"

Whatever you do, don't go down this road. If you're ever tempted to write a line like "*They've re-interpolated the quantum field transmission data and reverse-engineered the resulting Heisenberg matrix to calculate our vector*" — just remember that "*They've found us!*" is a much better line. It's easier to say, easier to remember, has much greater impact, and makes sense to everyone who hears it.

Capt. Jean Luc Picard (Patrick Stewart) and Dr. Beverly Crusher (Gates McFadden) gear up for some serious Treknobabble. (*Star Trek: The Next Generation*, 1987-1994)

It's also worth remembering that people's names in science fiction film can be as much a source of comedy as anything if you're not careful. Ixnys Zyxiz may look great on the page, but if the reader cannot read it, they'll dump your script in the trash before they get 10 pages in. The same is true for audiences when presented with names like Zorg or Gaxy or Billy Twoshoes — it's difficult to take anyone seriously, no matter how dramatic the situation, when their name is Ambassador Zorax, and science fiction films where the characters sport bizarre names typically fail miserably.

FORMAL SPEECH AND STREET SLANG

There has always been, and there will always be, formal speech and street slang, and there is a time and place for both. Formal speech dominates wherever there is a strict hierarchy, such as in a monarchy, a government, the military, religious institutions, or law enforcement and it is also the mainstay of professions such as medicine, academia, and the law. Each of these types of organisation have formal ways of greeting each other and for addressing members of the hierarchy according to relative status — whether you outrank them or they outrank you — and these ways are habit-forming even in informal situations. If you've ever been in the military you'll know that even after you de-mob, it's impossible to stop calling someone "Sir" when you've had it drilled into you!

Street slang, on the other hand, is much less formal. It isn't bred into a person quite as much as it's picked up as you go. Street slang is also subject to the vagaries of affiliation and circumstance. While they may have certain key words in common, a member of one social group, a gang for example, will often use a different set of slang words to describe things than a member of a rival gang. The same is true for people that live on the South side of town as opposed to the North. Additionally, street slang continually evolves and changes as new words gradually enter into daily use. This means that slang is often used within a group to stop outsiders from knowing what is being discussed. Typically we think of criminals using their own cant in case the police are sniffing around, and in my neck of the woods, Cockney rhyming slang was developed for just this reason. But equally true is that each generation of children develops their own argot that prevents parents and teachers from listening-in to their conversations.

Having said all that, where the two sides meet is in describing each other. We will always use slang — often very derogatory slang — to describe the people we report to or the people who are in power, just as those in power will use derogatory terms to describe those who are beneath them.

Alex (Malcolm McDowell) finishes his moloko and contemplates a bit of the old ultraviolence on some veck he viddied. (*A Clockwork Orange*, 1971)

Depending on whether your story is set in the past, present, or future, you need to make sure the terms they use are the correct ones. Anything other than present day or very Near Future and you should try to avoid using language or phrases that will seem out of place. Don't use current slang or common cultural references and don't refer to objects or gadgets that may well have been superseded. Hardly anyone refers to a Filofax anymore, and Rolodexes only exist in the offices of Hollywood agents. If your story is set in the past, then you'll need to do some research to find the right names for articles of clothing, drinks, modes of transport, and so on, and you can also find out how things were described in common language as well as at the courts of the kings.

In the Far Future, though, you have the choice to either use very generic speech in order to flatten things out, or you can go wild and invent slang terms and street argot for your world and the things in it.

You can have a lot of fun with this. In *Blade Runner* the cops used "cityspeak" — a mish-mash of Spanish, German, Japanese, and French, with some other stuff chucked in for good measure — to demonstrate how we have lost our identities under the onslaught of giant corporations and rampant globalisation. A similar idea was adopted in *Firefly*, where the end of war saw a Sino-American Alliance, which meant that Chinese became the common second language, and people will often slip between the two when speaking.

You can also invent slang expressions for everyday greetings or farewells or myriad other situations. In *Blade Runner* the Replicants are referred to by the cops as "skin jobs," in *Firefly* they use the expression "shiny" to denote something as being "cool." If your world has a lot of extraordinary stuff in it, then you can often alleviate that by juxtaposing very ordinary dialogue against it. In *Ghostbusters*, for example, when Spengler describes crossing the streams to Venkman he says "*Try to imagine all life as you know it stopping simultaneously and every molecule in your body exploding at the speed of light*" And Venkman replies, "*Right. That's bad. Okay. All right. Important safety tip. Thanks, Egon.*"

And some things will always ring true, no matter when your story is set. Clever people, or people with specific knowledge about something, always try to impress others. Remember Jeff Goldblum's Dr. Ian Malcolm in *Jurassic Park*? He wasn't "just" a mathematician, he was a "chaotician" and went to great lengths to impress Laura Dern's Dr. Ellie Sattler about Chaos Theory. It's also true that workers will always moan about bosses and bosses will always moan about workers and neither side think that they are paid enough and both think the other side are paid too much and no one ever likes authority.

CREATING AN ALIEN LANGUAGE

Language is what makes us what we are. We live and breathe it, we think and dream in it, it illustrates what we hear and describes our thoughts to others. If I ask you to imagine the sea, someone from the Caribbean will likely think of beautiful, clear blue water lapping against golden sands, whereas someone from Scotland may think of the North Sea, dark, cold and forbidding with huge waves crashing against rocky coastland. The same is true for snow. In the UK we think mostly of harsh snowstorms followed by grey slush. In the Chamonix Valley, France, it means skiing and snowboarding and *après ski* fun. But to an Eskimo, it can mean a multitude of things and there's a different word for each. Snow that's just fallen, snow that clings to your clothes, the crust on fallen snow, snow that can be carved, fine snow, and snow floating on water. Words are truly powerful things. The right words can inspire rebellion or keep the peace; if it didn't, then books wouldn't get banned and political correctness wouldn't blight our lives. Science without the right vocabulary to describe it might as well be magic; the law mystifies anyone who isn't a lawyer and every profession has its own jargon, in effect its own invented language.

But Language also divides us. George Bernard Shaw is said to have described America and England as *"Two nations divided by a common language"* — and if language makes us what we are, then two people speaking two different languages will be very different kinds of people, and those differences can be the source of enormous conflict. In English the saying goes *"It's your funeral"* — which basically means "Fine, do it your way, you're the one who will suffer when it all goes wrong." In Russia they have a similar saying — *"My vas pokhoronim"* — which loosely means "We will be around for your funeral" or "We will outlive you." During a party at the Polish Embassy in Moscow, Khruschev infamously used this saying in an offhand remark about the recent Hungarian uprising and the Suez Crisis, but it was translated literally as "We will bury you." There was outcry from the Western press and given the fear over the nuclear arms race at the time, it was assumed that Khruschev meant he was literally going to bury the West in some act of aggression. A mistake like this can be very dangerous in real life, but it's all grist to the mill for a writer. Prejudice based on conceptual differences due to language are commonplace in fiction and make for great conflict.

Creating an alien language — or any fictional language for that matter — may seem like a daunting task, but if you follow some basic rules it's fairly easy to come up with something convincing, and when done right, can add some real flavour to your story.

You ain't from around here, are ya boy? (*John Carter*, 2012)

Quick tips

Start with pen and paper. It's much easier to build quick notes and compare words this way than to spend endless hours crafting the perfect spreadsheet or document. Do that when you have real rules to work with. Always remember to store all of your rules and notes away safely and securely. Nothing is more terrifying or heartbreaking than losing work that you've painstakingly created over a long period of time.

Okay, the basic steps are:

Decide on a name

Usually it will, in some way, be related to the nationality of its native speakers. In *Avatar*, the Na'vi spoke Na'vi. In our world the French speak French, Germans speak German, Spaniards speak Spanish, but also Argentinians speak Spanish, Canadians speak French and English — it gets complicated. Keep it simple. Unless the story dictates that something more complex is needed, then if your people are called the Froom, have them speak Froom or Froomish.

Decide how you want your language to sound

All languages have distinctive sounds. Latin languages like Spanish and Italian have a more lilting and poetic feel to them than Germanic languages like English or German. Eastern European languages like Bulgarian or Russian sound vastly different to Western European languages like Portuguese, and Scandinavian languages and Asian languages are different again. Think about your language. Is it guttural and harsh, or soft and lilting? Does it flow easily with people speaking fast or is more staccato coming in short, sharp bursts.

Create the alphabet

This is where the fun starts, creating the letters that are used to make the words. You can use our alphabet if you wish, just think up new words and new names for things. But you can also use the Cyrillic alphabet or pictograms, like in Chinese or Japanese, or even a series of symbols such as Egyptian Hieroglyphics. You can mix and match or make up your own as you see fit, and you can have as few or as many letters as you want, and you'll also need some numerals to depict numbers. However, before you get carried away, it's worth remembering that you need to decide how to pronounce all the symbols and letters you come up with and possibly give them all a name. The more complex your language, the harder it is to fix it in your head and the more likely you are to confuse yourself when writing.

Create the lexicon

This is the vocabulary of words that make up your language. Right now we don't mean every word, just the basic building blocks, the common words like *I, a, it, and, the, but, they, them, he, she,* etc. Then start on the common verbs like *to go, to be, to have, to do,* and finally the common things that surround us — *earth, sky, water, air, food, arms, legs, eyes, bridges, horses,* and so on. You're aiming for a usable list of nouns, verbs, and adjectives, and maybe a few adverbs for good measure. Try to make your words easily pronounceable, you don't want to invent a language that even you cannot speak, and as far as possible make the words feel natural to say out loud, too many apostrophes or too many Z's, Y's, and X's will always feel false.

At this point it's a good idea to try for some simple proper names. Try for first and last names, family names and names for clans or tribes, then try country names and place names. Additionally your alien race may well have things that do not have an earthly equivalent so you will need to invent words for the crops they grow and the animals they keep and the vehicles they use and names for the mountains and the seas and all the other parts of your world. And don't forget to think of numbers. A good way of doing this is to design your currency and its denominations. This helps you to know what kind of coins/notes/beads etc. are needed to trade, and helps you to place a value on everyday items like food and clothing.

Create the grammar
Grammar is the set of rules dictating how your sentences are constructed. Many non-English languages create sentences by what we would term reversing the order of things. For example "My aunt's pen is on my uncle's table" in French would be *"La plume de ma tante est sur la table de mon oncle"* or "The pen of my aunt is on the table of my uncle." While you can freely use this kind of construction, you should aim to create some original rules as well to give your language an identity of its own. I remember with horror conjugating verbs in my school french lessons, but it's important to figure out how to do it for your own language. There need to be distinct similarities and differences between *I go, you go, he goes, she goes, we go*, and *they go*, and you'll need to decide on tenses — past tense, present tense, future tense, perfect tense — but don't go mad. Once again, "only as much as is necessary" is a good rule.

Decide on the plural form of nouns so that there is a difference between gun and guns. You could use a single letter, like our letter S but it might be more interesting to devise prefixes and suffixes that you can always use in other parts of speech. Think about how to make verbs into adverbs. In English we add *-ly*, so that *slow* becomes *slowly*, and *quiet* becomes *quietly*.

Start using it to translate
Using your basic building blocks, start to translate simple sentences. Things like "He has gone for food" or "I am walking to the shops," and slowly build up from there, refining your language and expanding your vocabulary as you go. In the same way that it takes time to learn a foreign language, it will take time before you can use your invented language quickly and without thinking. If you have sufficiently nerdy friends, you might try teaching it to them and practicing speaking it amongst yourselves — it's a great way of having conversations about people without them knowing.

This is just a quick primer on language creation, but it'll get you well on the way to a full-blown language of your won. There is much more to consider, though. We haven't touched on dialects or accents or regional variations, reduced alphabets, writing systems, or roots. But if you're interested, then Holly Lisle's *Create a Language Clinic* is a must-read.

A quick word about cheating languages

If creating a full language seems too much like hard work to you, then you have a couple of ways out of it.

1) If your story world has the right kind of technology at its disposal then the old "Universal Translator" stuffed in one ear can solve the language problem.

2) You could always use that hoary old trope that aliens learned the entire English language from TV or radio signals on the journey here. It's worked before and it'll work again, I'm sure.

3) In *Avatar*, although the Na'vi had their own language, the first humans had already taught them English by the time the story started. It's a bit of a cheat, but it meant there were very few scenes that needed subtitles.

4) Another worn old cliché, but one that is still very much in use, is that only one person in the film can understand the alien and they translate for everyone else. In *Star Wars*, the only person who can understand Chewbacca is Han Solo, but the rest of the characters — and by extension the audience — know what he is saying because of Han's comments.

DEALING WITH EXPOSITION

More than any other genre, I find that science fiction screenplays are awash with exposition, and science fiction writers, more than any other it seems, feel the need to explain everything to an audience. Now while I'm a big fan of being able to justify your technology and build a believable world, you just don't have to explain everything. Leave a little mystery and your story will be better for it. But when you do need to explain something to the audience, you need to bury it in the dialogue and action in such a way that the audience doesn't know it's being spoon-fed exposition. In the 1950s you might have been able to get away with a character sitting on the edge of a desk and spilling exposition by saying "*Well Bob, as you know...*" — but that kind of dialogue won't wash with today's cinemagoers. They are far more sophisticated and you have to work that little bit harder to hide the tricks of the trade.

A lot of how you deal with exposition depends on the kind of film you're writing. For example, *Pitch Black* is a monster movie set on another planet and *Star Wars* is really a heroic fantasy set in space. These kinds of films require little or no exposition because the action is what carries the stories. Conversely, a film like *Inception* needs a fair amount of exposition to set up the technology, the characters, the plan, their roles, and the consequences. There are a number of ways you can do this, but these methods have stood me in good stead over the years.

Argument is a good way of hiding exposition. Two characters arguing over a subject is a simple way of explaining something to an audience. While each person states their case what they are really doing is giving the audience information. For example:

<pre>
                JOHN
Stay with you

                BILL
But that doesn't explain
how Corey got rich. She's
not even a Kingston. Well
only by marriage.

                JOHN
'Cos when ol' man Kingston
died — suspiciously I might add,
though nothing was ever proven
— Junior inherited the lot,
then lost most of it in some
mining venture that went wrong.
Corey snagged most of what
</pre>

```
          was left when she divorced
          him and then it turned out the
          mining co was owned by her brother.

                    BILL
          Sheesh, no love lost there then.
```

You see? Without meeting her the audience knows that Corey is rich, ruthless and powerful and she made an enemy of her ex-husband. Now, to throw a different angle on it, you could have a third person interrupt with another opinion, like so:

```
                    ALEX
          Actually it was her
          brother-in-law, not her
          brother, and she testified
          that he had deceived her
          to scam Junior. Junior got
          most of his dough back and
          she took a handsome payoff
          by way of a thank you.
```

That puts a whole different spin on things again, doesn't it? Be careful, though — it's very easy for an argument to sound false, so avoid out-and-out shouting. Keep it conversational, maybe even playful. A joke is also a great way of hiding exposition in dialogue.

Game playing is another great way to hide exposition. A game of "Family Fortunes" would work well:

```
                    JOHN
          We asked 100 people
          "How does a woman from
          a nothing background get
          rich quick?"

                    BILL
          I dunno, she murdered
```

```
                    the old man, right?
                           JOHN
                    You answered murder, our
                    survey said... "Meh-meh" No!
                    It was not murder. Care to
                    try again?


                            BILL
                    She divorced junior though,
                    I know that.


                           JOHN
                    You say divorce, our
                    survey said... Bing! That's
                    right... divorce is the top answer!
```

Nice, huh? We learn the stuff we need to know but we're enjoying the explanation because of the delivery, it's fun and we can make guesses and laugh along.

The next technique is to **disguise** the exposition behind an unrelated action, a technique the late, great Blake Snyder coined "The Pope In The Pool" (buy his book *Save The Cat!* to find out why). With this method we have someone give us the expository dialogue against a backdrop of something bizarre that throws the audience. For example, in the TV series *Fringe*, in the early episodes Walter Bishop would be in his lab at Harvard explaining his scientific theory about the latest case, while milking a cow! At this point the audience isn't so much bothered about the exposition as wondering why he's milking a cow? And how did he get it in his lab? At Harvard! This is a great fun technique to use, but be careful — you can't always be cute about hiding exposition.

Sometimes just making the exposition a **dramatic turn** can do the trick. If someone's life is in danger, you can always have a character say to them "*Your life is in danger!*" and go on to explain why. It's odd, I know, but sometimes a character just has to come out and say these things. This is a usable version of what's known as "hanging a lantern" on it, a phrase used to describe a time when you have a giant plot hole or problem with your story, but it can't be fixed. You know it, and the audience will figure it out, so you point to it and make it obvious that it's there.

140

Cobb (Leonardo DiCaprio) imparts his wisdom to Ariadne (Ellen Page). (*Inception*, 2010)

The **teacher and pupil** is an ever-popular method, especially where you have a mentor character whom the protagonist spends time with. Similar to the argument method, it's essentially two people having a conversation, but in this case it is expected that some form of explanation is coming, so the audience will not mind. The obvious example of this is in *Star Wars* when Obi-Wan Kenobi is explaining The Force to Luke Skywalker. Luke doesn't know what it is and neither do we, so Obi-Wan explains it to Luke — and us — and everyone is happy.

Flashback as a way of explaining something has, for a long time, been frowned upon as being somehow lazy or a cheat. I have some sympathy with this. Explaining a character's motivation for revenge by having a flashback to his mother being murdered when he was a child is kind of lazy, but on the other hand a lot of great stories start somewhere then flashback to two hours earlier and tell the story through to come back to that point, so it has its place.

Montage is another way of using flashback, or even flashforward. Spinning newspapers, TV announcements, calendar pages turning, photos yellowing are all commonplace parts of a montage, and this technique often allows us to cover a fairly long period of time in order to set up the situation where our story will begin or will continue.

Finally we have **voice-over**. I'm not a fan, generally. Once again, I think it's lazy writing and film, as we're all constantly being reminded, is a visual medium. Show, don't tell. *Blade Runner* is an infamous case of a film not being helped by voice-over at all, and in later director's cuts the voice-over was removed.

A couple of things to remember. People don't talk about themselves, at least not unless they're a crushing bore. Your characters should reveal themselves to us in small ways, through action and through dialogue, and never through great gobs of self-explanatory exposition. The only time people talk about themselves is when they are little people and they are trying to make themselves seem big. Big people, on the other hand, never need to talk about themselves. Others will always do it for them. Big characters need no introduction, they just walk on and we instinctively know they are important.

The other thing to remember is that places and people can be described by simple actions rather than words. Alongside sight and sound, we have the senses of smell, taste, and touch, and we can always use these alongside a facial expression, movement, sigh or cry, to let the audience know what is going on. A wrinkled nose and a grimace often lets an audience know that something stinks much more effectively than dialogue stating it.

Overall the trick with exposition is to drip-feed the audience, only give them small pieces at a time as the story needs it, and let them join the dots on their own.

MAKING DESCRIPTION WORK HARDER

Script readers often complain about too much "black" on the page, meaning there's too much description and not enough dialogue. Often this is true, but we can't have no description, so what do we do? Well, if there's one single trick to better screenwriting, it's this; reduce every sentence down to its absolute essence, and use the fewest possible words to make the biggest possible impact. I've yet to read a screenplay without sentences that could be shorter or more succinct, especially my own! I am a long-winded gasbag when it comes to first drafts, and the first thing I always do on a re-write is start cutting down the word count. It takes practice and a ruthless approach, but finding precisely the right words makes your sentences shorter, faster, and easier to read.

So how do we do this? Well if I say to you "spaceship," some of you will imagine the Starship Enterprise, others will think of the Millennium Falcon, and others yet will picture the Nostromo. All different, but all basically comprising a series of corridors, a bridge, an engine room, crew quarters, a sick bay, etc. and all with airlocks, cargo bays, some kind of engine, a way to dock, a way to land — pretty standard stuff. Therefore, it's not necessary to describe the paintwork or the colour of the seat covers or the exact internal dimensions of the cargo bay. It's enough to write something like:

EXT. SPACE. YEAR 2122.
The giant mining ship Corinthian pushes relent-
lessly though the void.

That's it. We're done. That's all we need to describe our location. Everything else is implied in that one line and we don't need to embellish. The same is true when we move inside the ship. You could easily write:

INT. HYPERSPACE SLEEP BAY. CORINTHIAN
We hear the hiss of gas escaping as the first
chamber pops open.

Now this would work. We've all seen so many hyperspace sleep bays in films and on TV that a reader can probably picture the location, but occasionally you do need a few details, to generate atmosphere for example. So maybe we should try:

INT. HYPERSPACE SLEEP BAY. CORINTHIAN
Empty corridors. Darkness. Nothing moves. Blue
lights from a digital display wink on and off
until... a single RED light flicks on. The sharp
hiss of escaping gas shatters the silence and
Chamber One opens.

A little bit more, but not much more. Not too much, anyway. We've given our reader enough to set the tone of the piece and we've lent some atmosphere to our spaceship, but we haven't described every detail. The reader will fill-in those blanks for themselves. Now let's think about how we do this with character. Well, let's compare the sleeping quarters of these four captains:

```
INT. CAPTAIN'S QUARTERS. CORINTHIAN
Dirty laundry litters the floor, next to an over-
flowing ashtray. An empty whiskey bottle stands
upright on its neck, balanced on a stack of
files, whose stained and torn contents are strewn
everywhere.
```

```
INT. CAPTAIN'S QUARTERS. CORINTHIAN
Row upon neat row of leather-bound volumes lines
a wall of faux-oak shelves and an old telescope
sits next to a wingback chair by the only view-
ing window.
```

```
INT. CAPTAIN'S QUARTERS. CORINTHIAN
Spartan, white, every surface gleams. The furni-
ture is minimal, a chair, a lamp, a coffee table,
but each piece a design classic; form as well as
function.
```

```
INT. CAPTAIN'S QUARTERS. CORINTHIAN
A standard issue chair sits next to standard is-
sue table. On the table a standard issue mug
steams with coffee atop a standard issue coaster
while the standard issue slate beeps its standard
beep, announcing an incoming message.
```

Four short descriptions but four very different rooms. As you read you can picture everything about the occupant of each room straight away. We've simply made the room an extension of their personality and it says more than any amount of eyes, hair colour, age, rank, or uniform ever could. You can imagine what the bed looks like in room one can't you. And you can just picture what the captain is going to look like when we seem him laying on it. In room two there may well also be a bottle of whiskey, but you just know it will be a nicely aged single malt served in the correct glass, and all the while, in room three someone is fixing the perfect espresso, from the perfect beans using the perfect coffeemaker. Short, vivid details that imply other details is what you're shooting for, and the audience will fill in the blanks.

The same is true for describing a character — short, precise details that imply the rest. Often a single sentence can do the trick. If we read *"SHEILA MULLINS, face like a slapped arse,"* we can guess at exactly what she looks like, how she speaks, and how she behaves, long before we actually meet her. The same is true for *"JEFF REEVES, 32, born-too-late hippy,"* I can guess from that simple description his look, his clothes sense, his politics, his taste in music, and so much more.

But this is just "stuff" we're describing, and whenever possible we only want to describe "stuff that moves," so how about we try combining the room and the character and add some motion to the scene.

```
INT. CAPTAIN'S QUARTERS. CORINTHIAN
Tripping over his dirty laundry, CAPTAIN NICK
BUTCHER up-ends an overflowing ashtray, sending an
empty whiskey bottle crashing to the floor and a
stack of files with it.

INT. CAPTAIN'S QUARTERS. CORINTHIAN
Row upon neat row of leather-bound volumes lines
a wall of faux-oak shelves. Relaxing in a wing-
back chair, CAPTAIN PARDEW conducts Debussy with
one eye closed and the other glued to an old tele-
scope by the only viewing window.

INT. CAPTAIN'S QUARTERS. CORINTHIAN
CAPTAIN CRESSY, immaculate and crisply pressed,
stands to greet them in the centre of a spartan,
white cabin, every surface gleaming. Furniture is
minimal; chair, lamp, coffee table — each piece a
design classic — form as well as function.

INT. CAPTAIN'S QUARTERS. CORINTHIAN
In a standard issue chair next to standard issue
table sits CAPTAIN BILL REYNOLDS nursing a stan-
dard issue mug of steaming coffee. His standard
issue slate beeps its standard issue beep, an-
nouncing an incoming message.
```

The difference is immediate. We now know exactly what kind of person each captain is, reinforced with a description of his surroundings, and with the minimum of words. Now let's look at some other techniques to make description work harder.

Find precisely the right word

In a screenplay, no one ever just walks towards someone. They might *stroll* over to them, or *stampede* towards them, or maybe they *bounded* across to them, but they didn't just *walk*. They can *race* or *ramble* or *saunter* or *stride* or *march* or *diddy-bop* or *hike* or *prance* or *strut* or *tramp* or *stumble* or *plod*, but they never, ever just *walk*. It's not just about avoiding boring words, although that's part of it. The exact word you choose can describe the action far more precisely, helping with mood and tone, and it adds depth to the character.

It's also about using strong ACTIVE words. Avoid *starts to...* or *begins to...* or *tries to...* at all costs, and also avoid *-ing* words. *David walks* has far more power than *David starts to walk* or *David starts walking*.

Avoid cliché

Keep your description as fresh and original as you can, avoid worn out description such as *hourglass figure* and *beady eyes* and *fights like a tiger*. They're okay for a first draft, and we all do it, but when you go back for the re-write, replace them with something brilliant.

Avoid adverbs

This is an age-old warning that applies to just about every kind of writing. Readers, editors, and publishers all hate them, and they're easy to recognise, as they normally end in *-ly*, such as:

- He crept stealthily.
- She yelled angrily.
- He moved slowly.

It's weak and, as such, it lacks the impact or the tension we're looking for. So always re-write to remove adverbs:

- He creeps.
- She yells.
- His movement, slow.

Describe how something feels rather how it looks
We have five senses and at times it's better to evoke a sensation that the reader will identify with rather than try to describe something that may be hard to relate to. Some examples might be:

- Touch — It's skin is tough, leathery, and it's scales chafe against her skin.
- Taste — The metallic, coppery taste of blood tells him he's hurt (although that is itself a terrible old cliché).
- Smell — The air smells sweet, thick with jasmine, sandalwood, and vanilla.
- Sight — Sweat-soaked skin glistens like diamonds in moonlight.
- Hearing — His laugh is coarse, breathing and snorting like a braying donkey.

Use single word sentences
Breaking.
Sentences.
Into.
Single.
Words.
Draws.
Eyes.
Down.
A.
Page.

I've seen this work a couple of times, it's a neat trick but it's not for someone starting out unless they are supremely confident of their writing. You really need to be an established writer to get away with it.

Make your similes and metaphors unusual
We use similes to describe something by comparing it to something different, typically something like "*His teeth were grey and crooked like old tombstones.*" Try to find unusual comparisons to make your similes stand out. For example, "*He checks her out, subtle, like a crowbar.*"

Metaphors, on the other hand, are figures of speech where something is described as if it were something else completely. For example.

"*Jim is a thunderstorm*" or "*She's a butterfly, bright and gentle and stays nowhere long.*" It can also be used to describe activities — "*drowning in paperwork*" is a metaphor, as is "*the car ploughs through traffic.*"

As a rule of thumb, no single passage of action should be longer than four lines. You can fake it by breaking up longer paragraphs, with a character yelling something like *Behind you!* halfway through the action, but you can't get away with that every time. You can help the reader to enjoy description, however, if it's fun to read. An engaging and distinctive style will always help, but it's not something you can develop overnight. What you can do right away, though, is remember this; we are writing movies — moving pictures — so whenever we can we try to avoid describing the "stuff" in a scene, only the "stuff that moves." Even though, as a writer, you can picture every detail in your mind's eye, don't waste time writing it all down. It will just bore your reader and interrupt the flow of the narrative. It's also worth remembering that once the director, the production designer, the props guys, the set dresser, the editor and the VFX folks have all been through it, little of your original vision will remain, so only write what is necessary to convey the general feel for something, or the basic emotion of the scene.

Exercise Eight

~

Go back to the characters you created in Exercise Three and have them all sit in a circle and have a conversation.

During this conversation they will each explain how they came to be on the planet, and what they're most worried about now that the bad guys have taken over.

Remember the basics. Make sure that each of them has a distinctive voice. Give them accents or inflections that are personal to them and make sure they have patterns of speech that are unique. They won't all be nice to each other, either. Some of them will feel that they are more important than others and have more to lose. They may be scathing towards others or sarcastic about the things they say. The reaction from the rest of the group may be argumentative or belligerent. It may be equally scathing in return. Some of them may become protective of others. Some will try to lead, others will follow. The point is, they must be individuals, characters that you can tell apart from each other by actions, by attitude, by patterns of speech, and by vocabulary.

The proof of the pudding will be in reading your finished piece out loud. Can you tell who's speaking without their names at the top of their dialogue? Really? If you can, then great, but if you can't, then it's back to the drawing board and try again until you can.

Extra Credit

In the grand tradition of "learn by doing" that is writing, go through your own existing screenplay(s) and start to clean up your dialogue. You can do this in various ways, but start by just removing words like *and, then, was, but,* and see how much shorter you can make each sentence. Then go back and take out pairs like *starts to..., goes to..., begins to...* and see what impact that has. Next, remove redundant words and clichéd expressions and try replacing them with unusual metaphors and similes. Finally, start from scratch and do all three and see how dramatically your dialogue has changed from its original incarnation to how it is now.

.

CHAPTER NINE

START WRITING

❧

MOOD AND TONE?

Tone is how we usually describe the overall atmosphere of the writing, the emotional resonance it establishes and maintains throughout, and it reflects the writer's attitude toward the subject matter. Tone can be dark, pessimistic, bitter and twisted, or it can optimistic, light-hearted, funny and hopeful. It can also be celebratory, joyous, sophisticated, respectful, zany, and many other things.

Mood, on the other hand, is what the reader experiences in the writing, and mood is something a good writer will play with from scene to scene depending on whether they want to lighten the tone or darken it. Often you'll want to mirror the emotions of the point of view character, and occasionally you'll want to contrast with them, but usually the mood is filtered through what they see, feel, and hear. Even if they're not in the scene, mood is often set by their emotional state.

Along with genre, the tone of the piece should be crystal clear from page one. The opening of *Blade Runner* shows a dark, menacing landscape of massive industrialisation with great stacks belching flames hundreds of feet into the air. There's no mistaking the tone that's being set here. The same can be said for *Back to the Future*, as Marty McFly plugs in his guitar and we pull back to reveal a GIANT amplifier. When Marty hits that power chord and the resulting sound-wave sends him hurtling across the room, we know exactly what kind of movie we're watching.

It's imperative that you set the tone straight away. If nothing has happened by the end of page one and the reader still doesn't know what kind of script they're reading, you're in trouble. You have to paint a very vivid image of the tone right from the get-go. If it's a thriller they should be on the edge of their seat. If it's a horror they should feel afraid. If it's a comedy they should laugh. Thrillers and action films need to start quickly so they tend to use shorter, clipped sentences to increase pace. Romantic comedies and broad comedies often have a more leisurely, relaxed feel about them. Better yet, if you can introduce your main character with an anecdote and clearly articulate the tone, you're "home and hosed."

Don't be afraid to adopt a grim and gritty tone if the story needs it. No one will thank you if your script is bland in tone. If your characters are going to start dying as a result of an unknown and uncontrollable virus, then even if you start out with the family having breakfast together, there should be a dark undertone to the writing. Otherwise when bad things start to happen, the reader will be confused, especially if they went from family movie to post-apocalyptic horror with no warning.

A lot of screenwriters write stories that are a mix of two or three genres. If your screenplay has a genre mix, then the tone should reflect the balance of that mix. If it's an action/comedy, then is it an action movie with laughs or a comedy with action scenes? The tone needs to reflect that balance.

Finally, don't rush through your opening scene. In order to set the tone, give the reader a chance to settle into the fantasy world of your story before diving into the big events. Establish your setting, pick out some details, and then introduce the characters. You can even open with just sounds, keep the screen black, and then reveal what's making the sounds before getting to the setting and characters.

THE OPENING SCENE

Alongside setting the tone of your film, the opening scene has to introduce your main characters. More often than not you'll be introducing your hero, but it's not unusual to introduce the villain first to establish the problem and then introduce the man that, like it or not, is going to solve it.

There are many ways to do this, but the key here is to get the reader to care about, feel empathy for, and be worried about him or her well before you reveal any character flaws. An audience is going to be very unforgiving towards someone they neither know nor care about, but once they've established a rapport with the character and invested themselves emotionally in this journey, they will be able to forgive almost anything. How do you get the audience to invest? Well, putting the character in some kind of jeopardy will work, as will subjecting them to some underserved misfortune. Audiences also like characters that are highly trained or skilled in some specialised way, and of course characters that make us laugh or are just simply really nice people are easy to love.

Assuming the main character is going to have some kind of arc through the movie, then once you've established their personality you need to start demonstrating in what way they are broken so that we can watch them being fixed over the next two hours. Also, give your characters the breathing space to be properly introduced one at a time. Make sure they're described individually with unique actions and dialogue so that we get to know who they are. If you try to introduce them all at once, no one will ever remember who they all are or who the main character is.

Here's a few different techniques to open your screenplay:

A normal day

Exactly as it says, we open on a normal day in the life of our main character. We see them at work or at home, going about their normal routine, and we establish who they are and what they're like. When the inciting incident pulls them out of their routine, this is the life they are hoping to go back to.

Luke Skywalker (Mark Hamill) dreams of adventure. (*Star Wars*, 1977)

The starting point

We open with the main character at the exact point where the story starts. Maybe their ship just crash-landed on a remote planet, or maybe they just found out they're going to be a parent. Either way, this is where the adventure begins.

The foreshadowing event

Something happens before the timeline of our story that will ultimately effect its outcome. This technique is popular in end-of-the-world scenarios where the hero figures things out in time to save the day.

Dramatic irony

This is the name given to scenarios where the audience is privy to information that the hero does not have. This puts the audience in a position of authority, but because they know that this information will soon have a dramatic impact on the hero; it sets-up tension and anticipation.

The montage opening

A close cousin of the Foreshadowing event, the Montage is usually a number of close-ups of newspaper headlines, photographs, clippings, home movies, and so on, that tell the story-before-the-story, often covering a period of years.

The voice-over

For me, the least recommended of all openers (unless you're writing a *noir* detective story), but nevertheless an option. The narrator can be straight and true, or they can be unreliable, but their job is to give the audience a lot of context in a very short time, whether that's by explaining the present situation, the backstory, who the characters are, or all three.

THE FIRST 10 PAGES

The final thing that your opening scene must do is hook the reader. You have to grab them and pull them into the story so hard that they cannot put your script down. Over just one or two pages, that is very difficult. That's why every screenwriting book I've ever read and every class I've ever attended has hammered home the message that the first 10 pages of any script are the most important. Script readers, producers, actors, and agents are too busy to spend time reading every screenplay that comes their way all the way through, so your first ten pages have to make them keep reading and not stop until they get to FADE OUT. Easy to say, but how do you go about doing it?

In a nutshell, you have to provide compelling drama and an emotional experience.

Let's break it down into the constituent ingredients.

1) We have to **establish the genre** — in science fiction sometimes that's easy and sometimes it's not, but the reader must understand pretty immediately what genre they're reading.

2) **Establish the setting** — past, present, future? Which developmental stage is our world in? City or countryside, hi-tech or low-tech, alien or everyday?

3) **Set the tone** of the story — is it dark and gritty or light-hearted and whimsical? Is it comedy, drama, action, thriller? Is it bitter or hopeful?

4) **Introduce the main character** — we need to meet our hero and you need to make us care about them, empathise with them, and worry about them. This can be through an unjust misfortune or a stroke of bad luck or just because they're a nice guy, but they need to build rapport with the audience.

5) If it's an ensemble, we need to **meet any other key characters** — one at a time, with space to tell their own story, preferably via some kind of anecdote and with distinctive voices.

6) If it's necessary or possible, we can **meet the villain** — it's not always necessary or possible at this point, but usually within the first 10 pages we know what the hero is up against.

7) **Demonstrate the current status quo** — set the benchmark for how things currently are, the hero's day-to-day life, whether they're happy or discontent, etc.

8) **Point out the main character's flaws** — only AFTER we have established a rapport with the audience do we set up the hero's flaws, the fear or mental block or emotional scar that the hero is carrying around with them. This sets up the character arc so we can see how the hero must change by the end of the story.

9) **Illuminate the theme** — we absolutely must speak to the theme in some way. A question must be asked, the answer to which the story will try to explore. It can be implicit or explicit, but it must be presented to the audience.

10) **Set up the drama** — something needs to happen to get the story started. This will be story-specific as mysteries and thrillers take longer to set up than romances and comedies, but either way, something dramatic has to happen.

A few quick tips

- Don't waste time with lengthy exposition or trying to give us backstory. That stuff takes time and you cannot afford to wait until page 30 to get the real story started.

- You can't have people thinking about stuff. On screen people thinking about stuff = people standing around doing nothing except staring into space, so they need to be doing things.

- I have mixed feelings about this, but in general it's a bad idea to open with gratuitous sex or violence or with someone ranting away and screaming obscenities at someone else. Now I say I have mixed feelings about this because if the story justifies it, and it truly reveals something of character, then you can probably get away with it, and it does have shock value. The same is true for opening with a car chase or explosion.

- Your opening scene can take place over more than one location. If you open with a couple arguing in the bedroom, continue to the breakfast table, then continue in the car, then she kicks him out on the freeway. It's all one scene but it uses more than location. Clever use of this technique can make an opening scene very compelling.

- Figure out how your story is going to end. A lot of the initial work at the beginning of a screenplay has to do with foreshadowing events and setting up character arcs. If you don't know how the film is going to end then you don't know what events to foreshadow or how to initiate the character arc.

DON'T BORE THE READER

This is pretty self-explanatory, but if the story is only interesting to you then no one else will care about it. In order to make people care about it you have to find the emotional hook that will resonate with the reader. The best way to achieve this is to always remember that — as I've said before — like all stories, science fiction is first and foremost about people.

What follows is a list of the kinds of things that will bore a reader. Don't sweat the stuff you cannot control, the biggest being subject matter. Fact is, if the person reading your screenplay just hates science fiction, then nothing you will ever do is going to get them to change their mind. Move on. But absolutely make sure you work at the things you can control so they are the best they can be. In reality there is no one thing that will keep all readers interested at all times, but act on this list and it'll certainly help.

• **In the writing....**
Cut out all the unnecessary words
I have to tell you, this is me every time I write, very long first draft then hours of cutting and trimming. But it's worth it. The easiest words to trim are *then*, *and*, and *but*. In almost every case they are unnecessary and just add fat to the sentence. The next words you can usually trim are *that*, *really*, *just*, *quite*, and *perhaps*, along with *there is* and *there are*. Finally, cut the wordy phrases, things like *at this moment in time* when you should just say *now*, and *in the near future* instead of *soon*. Of course sometimes these words are needed, like in dialogue for instance, but most often they are not, so be ruthless.

Give your writing some style
Good writing has balance. No one wants to wade through over-flowery prose or read with a thesaurus open next to them, so keep the words simple and the sentences short. At the same time, yes you should cut as much fat as possible, but don't leave it looking like bullet points on a PowerPoint deck. The trick is to add some spice to the mix by adding something of your own personality to it. That means interesting similes, interesting metaphors, and some of your own local colour. Enough to be distinctively *you*, but without distracting from the story. Yeah I know, but no one said it was easy.

Don't overdo descriptions or details

Jeans and a red shirt is usually enough description, if it reveals something of character you could use *Jeans and a red Armani shirt*, that would be plenty. What you don't want is *Blue vintage Levis 501 red-tab jeans and a red Emporio Armani shirt, white canvas Chuck Taylor Converse All-Stars and a brown leather belt*. Balance in all things.

Use page-turners to keep the reader hooked

In the same way that a TV show uses cliffhangers to stop you switching channels during the commercial break, you can use page-turners to keep the reader interested in your script. I once had a main character return to his apartment with the words *"Honey, I'm home..."* — but followed up by saying *Giant arms knock him flat on his back and a huge, slathering, teeth-filled maw closes down over his face*. END OF PAGE. I mean come on, who's not going to turn the page when they read that? Of course it turns out to be his dog, which was funny, and it foreshadowed events later in the story, but no one who read that line didn't keep reading.

• In the story....
Choose an interesting idea

I'm not saying that a story about a man finding himself after going on a spiritual journey can't be entertaining, but if he escapes cannibal-pygmies, fights a mountain lion with his bare hands, and communes with alien beings from one of Jupiter's hidden moons on the way, then it'll be a far more interesting story. You need drama and conflict and action if your film is going to be entertaining to the masses, so pick subject matter that provides it.

Your main character must do things

Heroes don't stand around waiting for things to happen, they get out there and start making things happen for themselves. If your main character is standing around not doing anything, then your story is probably boring. There are exceptions to this rule, but not many.

Every scene must move the story forward

Very much related to having an active hero is putting them in scenes that move the story forward, or reveal something of character. Your hero needs a goal for the overall story, but in each scene, give your hero a smaller goal that counts towards the bigger goal. If they need to know something, then they find someone who can give them information. If they need to get somewhere and they don't have transport, then they're looking for transport. Always moving forward is the golden rule.

Don't write random action or have fuzzy motivation

Very much the cousins of "always moving forward" are making characters do something random that is never mentioned again, something that's against their character type, does nothing for the story and is just filling up pages. For all the good things that I enjoyed about Prometheus, it had several scenes like this, most notably when a physically ravaged Fifield returns to the ship and proceeds to kill half a dozen crewmembers before being flame-throwered to death by Vickers. It's a big scene of action and CGI that results in a lot of deaths, a lot of damage, and a lot of mayhem, but afterwards no one mentions it, not even in passing.

The stakes must be clear

What happens if the hero fails? If we don't know or don't understand, then we don't care, and you want us to care. Make sure the stakes are as high as they can possibly be for your character. Will he lose his children? Will the Earth be destroyed? Will he not get the job? The stakes must be as high as they can possibly be for your character, then we will care whether he succeeds or fails.

Have interesting characters

It sounds kind of obvious, but even if you get everything else right, if your characters are dull and if we don't care enough about them, then your story will ultimately fail. They must be properly introduced, have a unique voice, and we have to like them.

Don't be obvious

Make your screenplay fresh and exciting by being original. Whatever your first choice for a scene or a character or the plot, it's probably been done before. Spend time trying to find the new way to do things, the new location, the new dialogue, the new plot development. What's the action scene we've never seen before? What's the weapon or technology or gadget that's never been used in a film before, or better yet, never existed outside of your imagination. How can we throw in a twist or a reversal that no one saw coming? It doesn't always have to be *"Luke, I am your Father..."* — it can be *"I love you"* *"I know"* — but the more unexpected it is the better.

Vary the pace

Relentless action or horror or drama can be draining, and often isn't very interesting to watch. Action movies need quiet moments, dramas need comic relief, so remember to keep the flow of your movie dynamic, give it ups and downs to let the audience catch their breath.

DON'T BAFFLE THE READER

This is kind of self-explanatory but here goes; your reader doesn't care about the science in your film. I know, right? But to be fair, they're on their thirtieth screenplay for that week and they're tired and hungry and they've got an hour's drive home and they've had a row with their boyfriend about the hours they're doing and frankly the last thing they want to read is your story of the death and destruction of planet Earth at the hands (mouths?) of giant space eels. So you need to make it compelling and dramatic and exciting, and no matter how cool the rest of your ideas are, if you baffle the reader with science, you'll lose them. Providing you've followed the rest of the guidelines in this chapter, then you need to remember these simple rules:

Don't use too much jargon

The occasional three-letter acronym is fine for military or scientific purposes as long as it's obvious what is actually going on, but don't launch into long explanations of the physics of action/reaction systems for propulsion during space travel.

Don't expect the reader to understand anything

In fact, assume the reader is a fine art major with a minor in film and has no clue about maths, physics, chemistry, biology, or anything else that might be on your mind while writing your masterpiece. They don't know and neither should they.

Don't assume they know the same things as you do
You might well be fascinated with space travel, nanotechnology, archaeology, crop circles and the medieval mind, but there's a very strong chance that the reader won't be. If you're using specialist knowledge in your screenplay, then don't skimp when explaining it to others — especially the audience — and don't assume they'll have heard about any of the things you're talking about.

Don't get overly technical
Very much related to the first two, you're not writing a technical manual or an academic paper. If they have to resort to Wikipedia while reading, then your story doesn't work and you need to simplify it or find a way to make it easier to understand.

It's not a novel
As the old saying goes, *"If it ain't on the page, then it ain't on the stage."* You don't have the luxury of long backstories or seeing into the mind of your hero and knowing what he's feeling, and you can't stick a map on the inside cover so that readers can follow all the locations. Keep it visual and simple and easy to follow.

EXERCISE NINE

Below are the first ten pages of an example screenplay. It may not be the best writing in the world, but read through it and see if you can pick out each of the 10 things that must be addressed in the first 10 pages of a screenplay. To refresh your memory, these first ten pages should:

1) Establish the genre.
2) Establish the setting.
3) Set the tone.
4) Introduce the main character.
5) Meet any other key characters.
6) Meet the villain (if necessary/possible).
7) Demonstrate the current status quo.
8) Point out the main character's flaws.
9) Illuminate the theme.
10) Set up the drama.

Above all, it must have enough going on that the reader doesn't want to put it down. There has to be enough excitement, imagination, intrigue, mystery, suspense, etc., to keep the reader turning the pages past page 10, all the way to the end.

———————————— PAGE 01 ————————————

FADE IN:

INT. TROOPSHIP TRANSPORTER. SPACE

TROOPERS ready themselves for work. An under-current of serious professionalism despite the insults and macho banter led by the loudest of them, JACK TRANTER.

TROOP SERGEANT DRISCOLL turns from his discussion with TROOPER BARRA to face them.

> DRISCOLL
> Gentlemen, listen up. We have yet
> another abandoned freighter, no
> signs of life and, I expect, picked
> clean like the others.

> TRANTER
> That's four in what, seven weeks?

> DRISCOLL
> Yep, but ours is not to question
> why. Those awfully clever people
> over in 'intelligence' can figure
> that out, as usual we're just the
> salvage team.

> TRANTER
> Twenty million euros of training to
> become the intergalactic triple A.

There's a collective laugh.

>   DRISCOLL
>   Okay settle down, I want nothing
>   complicated, no heroics. The rats
>   have left the sinking ship so let's
>   fire it up and get it home.

>   BARRA
>   Check your gear, we dock in 6
>   minutes... and be prepared to walk.

Everyone groans at this last comment.

>   BARRA (CONT'D)
>   Enough! We may be precautionary
>   measures only but you are
>   professional soldiers. Now act
>   like it.

TRANTER flips open a stainless steel hip flask,
offers it to Trooper BARRA.

>   BARRA (CONT'D)
>   Jesus, Jack. Now is not the time.

PAGE 02

>   TRANTER
>   You get more like my Mom every day.
>   It's just an iso-drink.

He raises the flask in a toast.

>   TRANTER (CONT'D)
>   The lowest bidder.

Tranter takes a hit. Barra smiles, shakes his head. Other TROOPERS exchange looks then get seriously interested in the condition of their gear as the -

TROOPSHIP

- banks right and we pull back to reveal the FREIGHTER, motionless. No lights. No sign of life. The troopship PILOT checks monitors, dabs a couple of buttons.

                    PILOT
        This ship supposed to be dead?

                    DRISCOLL
        According to intel, Why?

                    PILOT
        I'm getting very low-level vital
        signs. Indeterminate origin.

                    DRISCOLL
        Fabulous. Any response?

                    PILOT
        Negative. No RTD response. Could be
        the ship's cat or something, but...

DRISCOLL turns back to the TROOPERS. They stand as one and snap into readiness.

                    DRISCOLL
        You heard the man, looks like we're
        walking. Standard two-plus-two
        formation, one man always secure.
        We're too far out to chase after
        floaters. Barra, you and Tranter
        are on point.

                        BARRA
          Sir!

The two men move to the front of the group and
ready the airlock doors.

                    BARRA (CONT'D)
          Airlock prepped. Good to go sir.

———————————————————— PAGE 03 ————————————————————

                      DRISCOLL
          Opening inner airlock on my mark. 3
          2-1 mark.

The airlock door slides open and the team makes
its way into the small chamber. BARRA and TRANT-
ER prep the outer door.

                        BARRA
          Outer door prepped and ready sir.

DRISCOLL lifts his wrist to his mouth and speaks
deliberately into his sleeve.

                      DRISCOLL
          Seal inner door.

The inner door slides shut. He turns to face the
outer door.

                  DRISCOLL (CONT'D)
          Crosscheck seals and O2.

Each man checks his buddy's helmet and gauges.

One TROOPER whispers to his partner.

                    TROOPER
I will never get used to this shit.

                    DRISCOLL
Let's do this thing.

                    BARRA
Opening outer doors. 3-2-1.

A LOUD HISS and the outer doors slide apart. Men brace themselves against the rush of escaping air pulling them into the dark void.

EXT. TROOPSHIP TRANSPORTER. SPACE

BARRA and TRANTER stand on the threshold eyeing the distance to the silent FREIGHTER. A LOOK, and wordlessly they play rock, paper, scissors.

                    TRANTER
Oh man! Best of three?

                    BARRA
In your dreams.

BARRA secures a harness to the TROOPSHIP. TRANTER hands the clip from his suit to BARRA and watches as he attaches them to each other, testing the join with a quick tug.

TRANTER sets himself for the jump between ships. Weighing the lifeline that connects him to his buddy he mutters under his breath....

            TRANTER
The lowest bidder.

...then pushes-off for the FREIGHTER DOOR. He
cushions his impact against the hull, steadies
himself, secures his suit to the door and signals
to BARRA.

BARRA unclips himself from the troopship, checks
the buddy line to TRANTER and pushes-off. He
lands next to TRANTER, grins and SILENTLY
MOUTHS.

            BARRA
  Touchdown.

TRANTER hacks a KEYPAD outside the giant
freighter and it's enormous double doors grind
open. Weapons drawn, they peer inside for signs
of life. Nothing. BARRA signals the team to
cross.

INT. ABANDONED FREIGHTER. SPACE.

Doors shut behind them, TRANTER's face glows
blue from the monitor he is studying.

            TRANTER
02 looks good.

            DRISCOLL
You sure? Why no power?

            TRANTER
Dunno Sarge. According to these
readings there's adequate power at
the generator and 02 is good.

                    DRISCOLL
        How sure?

TRANTER looks at him and then at BARRA.
BARRA shrugs. TRANTER sighs and, looking at his
gauge, flips off the O2 supply then grips under
his helmet and twists.

Suddenly he DROPS TO HIS KNEES, GASPS FOR AIR,
GRABBING AT HIS THROAT. BARRA CRIES OUT, rushes
over, but stops. TRANTER's shoulders are shaking. He tips his head back...laughing!

                    BARRA
        You motherfu...What the fuck man,
        that's not funny!

TRANTER is laughing out loud. The rest of the
troopers cuss him out and unfasten helmets.
TRANTER grins.

                    BARRA (CONT'D)
        I'm going to slap you so fu...

─────────────────── PAGE 05 ───────────────────

                    DRISCOLL
        Alright, alright. TRANTER, stop
        fucking about we've got a job to
        do.

TRANTER pulls himself up still smiling.

                    TRANTER
        Yes sir.

                    BARRA
        Shitbag.

                    TRANTER
I'm sorry man, I just couldn't
resist it.

                    BARRA
Fuck you. It wasn't funny.

                    TRANTER
Oh come on.
                    BARRA
I mean it. You can't keep fucking
about your whole life.

                    TRANTER
Really?

                    BARRA
Yeah really. Listen, sooner or
later you are going to have to grow
up. What are you going to do when
it's not just your life you're
fucking with? When it's your troop,
or your family?

                    TRANTER
Okay, I get it, you're pissed off,
I'm sorry.

                    BARRA
No. You don't get it. That's the
point. You never seem to get it.

BARRA pushes past TRANTER with the rest of the
troop. TRANTER gazes after them, frowning.

Quick and silent they swarm through the mazey
corridors. TRANTER keeps pace alongside BARRA. A
TROOPER calls out.

                     169

TROOPER
I got life. Less than 50 yards up
and to the right.

———————————— PAGE 06 ————————————

DRISCOLL
Okay you two, go and earn your
keep.
They ready weapons and move ahead. Carefully,
but with pace, using hand-signals to cover each
other round corners and through doors.

They reach an open crew cabin and position themselves either side. TRANTER pushes open the
door. No response. He takes in the room with a
glance.

TRANTER
Hamsters.

BARRA
What?

TRANTER points to an empty cage on a table in
the room.

TRANTER
Hamsters. Or rodents of some kind.
That's probably the life we've been
picking up. It might also be the
reason we've got no juice.

BARRA
Makes sense.

BARRA raises his sleeve to his mouth.

> BARRA (CONT'D)
> All clear Sarge, but it looks like
> we have a rodent problem.

Back with the group, DRISCOLL takes it in and
frowns.

> DRISCOLL
> So it's either fried itself in the
> frame somewhere or gnawed through a
> couple of wires.
> TRANTER
> That's about it, yeah.

> DRISCOLL
> Fucking great. What kind of asshole
> takes a rat into space anyway.

> BARRA
> Probably smuggled aboard. It's not
> unusual for folk to keep pets on
> long-haul gigs.

> DRISCOLL
> Okay, take two men, follow the
> cables to the engine room.
> If it checks out, give the
> machinery a once-over and report
> back.

—————————————— PAGE 07 ——————————————

BARRA nods and he and two men take off down the
corridor.

> DRISCOLL (CONT'D)
> Tranter.

                    TRANTER
        Sarge.

                    DRISCOLL
        Take two and head for the flight
        deck. Between us let's get this show
        on the road. I'll talk to our
        PILOT, see if we can give this
        thing a jump.

TRANTER and his men head off as DRISCOLL speaks
into his comms.

INT. FLIGHT DECK ABANDONED FREIGHTER. SPACE.

TRANTER crawls under a nav-console, torch in
mouth, eyeing a run of cables packed into the
trunking. A click of static and a voice comes
over his radio.

                    BARRA (O.S.)
        How's it going up there? Anything?

                    TRANTER
        Nothing yet, I'm tracking... no,
        wait a minute.

He pulls the severed ends of a cable from the
mass of wires in front of him.

                    TRANTER (CONT'D)
        I may have found the break.

                    BARRA (O.S.)
        What is it?

                    TRANTER
        No idea, but I'll fix 'em together
        and see if it works.

INT. ENGINE ROOM ABANDONED FREIGHTER. SPACE.

BARRA stares at a mass of pipework connecting two giant engines that dominate his view. He turns his head sideways as something catches his eye underneath them.

─────────────── PAGE 08 ───────────────

                    BARRA (REPLIES INTO HIS RADIO)
          Okay. Careful what comes on, it's a
          real mess in here.

BARRA calls another trooper over, points.

                    BARRA (CONT'D)
          What do you make of that?

                    TROOPER
          Not sure, but someone's tampered
          with these drives. There're re-routes in
     some hoses, almost as if
          they tried to sabotage them, but
          gave up.

                    BARRA
          Maybe they did. See if you can
          figure out what that is.

On comms.

                    BARRA (CONT'D)
          Sarge.

                    DRISCOLL (O.S.)
          What's up Barra?

> BARRA
> Tranter may have found the fault,
> he's fixing it now, but these
> engines look (beat) wrong. We
> should maybe think about a tow.

> DRISCOLL
> Okay, I'll head back and talk it
> out with HQ. Driscoll out.

INT. FLIGHT DECK ABANDONED FREIGHTER. SPACE.

> TRANTER
> Okay give that a go.

A TROOPER flips a couple of switches on the main
console. Little by little, lights flicker into
life around the flight deck.

> TRANTER (CONT'D)
> Nice.

He flips on the comms and as he speaks his voice
fills the entire ship.

> TRANTER (CONT'D)
> Welcome aboard flight FUBAR one,
> I'm pleased to announce we have
> juice.

———————————— PAGE 09 ————————————

INT. ENGINE ROOM ABANDONED FREIGHTER. SPACE.

BARRA looks up at the sound and shakes his head
grinning. He raises his communicator.

> BARRA
Everything look cool?

INT. FLIGHT DECK ABANDONED FREIGHTER. SPACE.

TRANTER looks over at the two troopers. They look back at him with thumbs up.

> TRANTER
Looks good here.

INT. ENGINE ROOM ABANDONED FREIGHTER. SPACE.

> BARRA
Okay, fire her up, I guess.

> TRANTER (O.S.)
Brace yourselves.

Twenty yards away, a TROOPER spots RED LIGHTS blinking on and off where the two engines meet. He frowns and bends to get a proper look. Another RED LIGHT. Lots of BAD WIRING.

> TROOPER
Hey! Come and look at this!

BARRA walks over, inspects the new wire.

INT. FLIGHT DECK ABANDONED FREIGHTER. SPACE.

> TRANTER
Firing in three.

INT. ENGINE ROOM ABANDONED FREIGHTER. SPACE.

> TRANTER (O.S.)
Two.

BARRA's eyes widen as it hits him.

                    BARRA
        Oh shit! Everyone out! It's a bomb!
        Run!

THREE TROOPERS turn and start running. BARRA is
shouting into his communicator.

                    BARRA (CONT'D)
        Stop! Don't fire the....

Too late.

──────────────── PAGE 10 ────────────────

INT. FLIGHT DECK. ABANDONED FREIGHTER.

                    TRANTER
        One.

TRANTER, oblivious to the danger, thumbs the
green button that starts the launch process.

INT. ENGINE ROOM. ABANDONED FREIGHTER.

                    BARRA (O.S.)
        It's a trap! The engines are
        rigged this whole thing is....

He doesn't get to finish his sentence. An explosion rips through the engine room and the hull
starts to breach.

                    BARRA (CONT'D)
        Suits! Now!

BARRA instinctively locks his helmet down just
as BAM! The hull rips apart, a TROOPER sucked

into space, out of sight. The other grabs a hand
hold as the room equalises.

INT. FLIGHT DECK. ABANDONED FREIGHTER.

               TRANTER
  What the..?

He grabs the microphone, but before he can speak
the whole ship shakes. The three TROOPERS look
at each other.

               TRANTER (CONT'D)
  Greg! Greg! Shit. You two, suit up
  now and get back to the transport.

               TROOPER
  What about you?

               TRANTER
  Get it fired up and wait for me,
  I'll meet you there as soon as.

Tranter grabs his things and sets off running,
fastening his suit as he goes.

———————————————— END ————————————————

With the exception of point 6 (introduce the villain), which we
don't have to do in this story, I think it pretty well covers all the bases.

But what do you think?

Feel free to rip it apart and improve on it if you think you can. As
I said, it's not an Oscar winner and writing is re-writing after all, but if
you can read it, tick off all of the points on our list and be interested in
what happens next then you've done your job.

Extra Credit

Go back to Exercise Three and write the opening 10 pages of our ter-raforming story. Set the tone and the mood of the piece, ensuring that the audience knows that bad stuff is going to happen. Describe what terraforming is to the audience through dialogue and introduce your characters and set up their personalities and attitudes to us.

Extra Extra Credit

Choose a different tone of voice completely and re-write the piece in that style. Try for a comedy or a family drama and see if they read like two completely different movies.

CHAPTER TEN

WHY STOP AT WRITING?

THE FUTURE IS NOW

I know you hear this a lot, but really, it's never been easier to make a film. The greatest power that the Internet has placed in the hands of people is the ability to communicate globally and to find others who share your ideals, your dreams, your vision. Harnessing that collective energy in the right way empowers you, gives you the ability to finance, crew, cast, shoot, edit, and distribute your film in a way that only a few short years ago was almost impossible. Couple that with ready availability of powerful computers and cheap software and there really is no excuse anymore. If you want to make movies, you can.

LO/NO-BUDGET SCIENCE FICTION

If nothing else, I hope that what you have taken away from reading this book is that great science fiction is not all about aliens, space travel, or mutant monsters. I say this because if you're working with a low- or ultra-low budget, then you need to cut your cloth according to your purse, and this means stories that are a bit more — literally — down to Earth.

One way of doing this is embrace the Mundane SF Manifesto that I mentioned right at the beginning of this book. This means no aliens, no space travel, no alternate universes, in fact nothing "fantastical" at all. Rather you explore the near future and the topics that will affect everyone, such as climate change, over-population and genetic engineering. If *Fahrenheit 451* can build an entire world around something as seemingly simple as the banning of books, think what you could do around a subject like anti-terrorism laws and the total erosion of our civil liberties in the name of freedom.

The other thing to do is look at the world around you and imagine change, imagine something big happening. *Children Of Men* was set in 2027 — not that far away — but in a world where we could no longer have children. Imagine then, in that world, the significance of a single pregnant woman. The world of science fiction is awash with other similar ideas that have yet to make it to the big screen. Here are a few:

- What if a sickness turned everyone over the age of 15 into raging zombies?
- What if all humans died by the time they reached 25?
- What if all four-legged animals started to die?
- What if all plant life started to die out?
- What if humans everywhere suddenly stopped dying?
- What if a new ice age decimated everything above the Tropic of Cancer?
- What if someone found a cure for cancer and gave it away?

All of these ideas are about the impact on society of enormous change, both technological and natural, and these are the big-issue themes to explore when writing. But your hooks into the story, like always, are your characters — ordinary people, with everyday problems, that we can all relate to.

It never fails to amaze me what can be done with little or no money and time, and for some fantastic examples of the genre take a look at the top films — including the winners — of the SCI-FI-LONDON 48-Hr Film Challenge over at http://www.sci-fi-london.com/webtv. Each team was given a title, a prop they had to include, and a line of dialogue they had to use and only 48 hours to finish a 5-minute short. Over the last three years the quality bar has just gotten higher and higher, which shows that teamwork, imagination, and a modicum of talent will get you a lot further than an unlimited budget.

There are plenty of examples of great science fiction films made for very little money. Even feature films can be produced on a shoestring if you put your mind to it. Don't believe me? Well check out *Monsters, The Man From Earth, Primer, Repo Man, Pi, The Girl From Monday, The American Astronaut,* and *Dark Star.* These are just a few examples of what can be done when you stop wishing for what you don't have and start using what you've got around you.

And you're not alone. There are many small but dedicated groups of filmmakers all over the world, organised into groups or clubs or meet-ups, all striving to make films together. You may find yourself doing sound on one film and acting in another in return for your chance to get your film made, but the implicit promise in all this is that if anyone has any success, they will bring the crew they worked with along on their next film — the one where you actually get paid!

Bottom line is that people want to make films, so try and write films that people can easily make. That doesn't mean limiting yourself or your imagination, but rather tailoring your work to fit that requirement. Once you have a couple of produced films under your belt, then that success will allow you to dream a bit bigger — and then you can go and write *Transformers 9: Back To Cybertron*. (But really, please don't.)

CROWDFUNDING AND CROWDSOURCING

We live in a connected age, more connected than at any other time in history. We are all a simple mouse-click away from literally millions of others around the globe who share our thoughts, ideas, and visions. Right now it's easier than ever to exploit this connectedness and make your own film by **crowdfunding**, using the power of the crowd to fund your endeavour, and **crowdsourcing**, using the power of the crowd to source talent, tools, knowledge and resources that will help you execute on your idea.

Both of these movements have seen astonishing success. *Iron Sky,* a darkly comic Finnish/German/Australian co-production about Nazis who fled to the dark side of the moon after WWII and have now returned to reclaim the Earth, raised nearly 20% of its final budget through some 200,000 fans built up across YouTube and social networking sites as well as its own film website. But as with all success stories, behind the scenes a lot of hard work and planning went into making it happen. There are some fabulous in-depth articles on this new phenomenon online, but here are a few basic tips and tricks to get you started.

Crowdfunding

As of this writing you cannot incentivise a crowdfunding campaign by offering financial rewards such as stock or shares or equity. This is because the financial machinery wants to control how and where you can invest your money — it's easier to tax that way — and while they're quite happy for you to become a legitimate VC or blow your pension on Apple stock, they don't want you investing a dime with someone you know personally who wants to write an iPhone app, manufacture a product, author a book, or make a film. This will change. There is already a groundswell of public opinion that wants a change to the law, but in the meantime you can only offer VIP "perks" as incentive to your audience, usually banded across different donation points.

In some ways I think this is actually the best thing about crowdfunding. There's nothing ambiguous about the promise, no outlandish financial claims, it's a simple *"You give us this amount and we'll say thank you by giving you this thing"* — but the argument goes that offering a possible financial reward will persuade more people to invest so bigger things can be done, but it will also open the floodgates for fraudsters and criminals which could well have the effect of scaring people away. We'll see. But in any case, how do you prepare for your campaign?

Step 1 — Planning

The old adage of *fail to plan and you plan to fail* was never so true. Putting together a successful crowdfunding campaign means meticulous planning, in-depth research, and a decisive call to action. You need to know, to the tiniest detail, what your story is, why people should back you, your financial goals, how long it might take to achieve, the number of reward levels you will have, what the rewards will be, and how you're going to stay engaged with your investors even after the film is made. Make no mistake, this could take as long as six months by the time you've budgeted. Set up a website, a blog, a Twitter account, Facebook pages, mailing lists, and all the other million and one admin duties you will have to perform along the way.

Don't go into this lightly. You're a professional and you need to approach crowdfunding in a professional way. You wouldn't go to a bank with a half-assed idea and ask for $100,000 to make a movie. You'd be laughed out the door. So don't think that you can approach crowdfunding in any less professional a manner just because the Internet is full of dancing kittens and pornography.

Step 2 — The Money

Asking for money is always hard. Seriously, how often do you just go up to strangers with your hand out and ask for a spare five dollars? But you can do it if you have a budget and a plan. So how much? Well, you need to start budgeting. Now I'm not about to start a crash course in film financing here, but you need to cover at least:

1) The cost of making the film (cast, crew, kit, production costs, etc.)
2) The cost of the rewards (t-shirts, hats, badges, posters, etc.)
3) The cost of marketing (mailing list, web hosting, etc.)
4) Incidentals (postage and packing, shipping, etc.)

Once you know how much this is you can decide whether you're going to try for all of it, some of it, or run a staged campaign where you get enough to go and make the film and then later on, once you have a kick-ass trailer, ask for some more to finish it. The key is to pick a funding goal that's large enough to get you making your film, but small enough that it can be confidently reached or exceeded. It's worth noting that the size and strength of your social network will directly affect your ability to reach your target, so be realistic about what you can achieve. The taint of a failed campaign tends to hang around a project.

So how long? Well, for a small project, 30 days seems to be about the norm and 70 days seems to be a good number for large amounts, but I've seen campaigns that last for 90 days. Be aware, though, that long campaigns lose momentum very quickly, so you need to be really engaged to make them work. It's better, I think, to give yourself a deadline, like a shoot date, and rigidly stick to it so you don't fizzle out.

Step 3 — The Rewards

Most successful campaigns seem to offer between 3 and 8 levels of reward. There's no hard and fast rule about what the rewards should be, but you need to not only be realistic about what you can offer, but very specific about what a reward entails. Popular examples of rewards at different levels look something like this:

- $5 gets a cool desktop wallpaper, your name on the credits, and our eternal gratitude.
- $10 gets the wallpaper, the credit, and a digital download of the film.
- $25 gets all that plus a beautiful eBook containing artwork and storyboards from the film.
- $50 gets all the above plus access to video extras such as "making of" featurette and cast and crew interviews.
- $75 gets all that in a beautifully packaged limited edition Blu-ray of the film signed by cast and crew.
- $100 gets all of the above plus a limited edition t-shirt of the movie artwork.
- $250 gets all the above plus a limited edition signed comic book of the film.
- $500 gets all the above plus one hour of script mentoring.
- $1,000 gets all these goodies plus your credit upgraded to Associate Producer and an invite to the premiere and afterparty.
- $3,000 all the above plus a set visit and dinner with the cast.
- $5,000 all the above plus a VIP pass to any film festival where we're exhibiting, invites to all the parties and a car to and from your hotel or wherever you're staying.
- $10,000 all the above and a tiny walk-on part in the film

Now let's analyse this cornucopia of goodies.

In case you haven't noticed, the first four pledges don't use any packaging or physical media, therefore no postage, therefore they're cheap to produce and send out. You don't want to be incurring any costs on pledges of $50 and under as that's where the bulk of your money will come from. Above the magic $50 marker you have to start producing t-shirts, Blu-ray discs, and a comic book. These things cost money to design, print, manufacture and mail out to people, so it needs to be financially viable to do so. To keep costs down make the t-shirts single colour (white on black always looks good) and if you're smart you can often do deals with suppliers so that they print their name at the neckline on the back of the shirt and in return you get the t-shirts at cost, or very close. Similar deals can be done with print and manufacture of discs, cases, and covers, so push for them.

If you're going to offer comic books, then you need to have contracted someone to do one. Often the storyboard artist and scriptwriter can be persuaded to create this between them, but they will want you to pay — even if it's just emotionally — for the privilege. What I'm really saying is if you're going to offer these nice add-ons to the film, then you have to know how you're going to supply them and how much it will cost.

From $500 to $10,000 what you're asking people to do is give up their time and be nice to someone who is paying hard earned cash so you can make films for a living. Low-budget productions should be used to having to do this, but make sure everyone is prepped to do the best job they can of making people feel wanted. To be fair the number of people who will pledge this type of money is very, very small, but the one or two that do should be appreciated. Do be aware though that none of these visit/party type rewards includes travel or accommodation. You should stipulate this in the terms and conditions of the pledge so that a guy living in Des Moines who pledges $1,000 doesn't expect to also get plane tickets to London and a weekend in a hotel when it comes time for the premiere.

Step 3 — Engaging The Audience

If you do nothing during your crowdfunding campaign then that's exactly what you'll get out of it — nothing. The most successful campaigns are the ones that are fed and watered regularly to keep potential investors engaged, excited, and up-to-date with everything that's going on. This starts with your video. You knew that, didn't you? You have to have a video!

You see the crowd isn't really interested in your project, or at least they're only peripherally interested in your project. What they're really buying into is you. Your passion. Your story. To do that they need to see your face, to look into your eyes and see the fire burning in you. That doesn't mean a great trailer — although that helps — no, they want the people behind this so they can get some sense of knowing what they're about. Quick tips for your video include:

- If it suits the mood, then try to be fun and original. It doesn't have to be perfect if it works and if you can make something that goes viral, then your chances of success are much increased.

- Look at the camera and tell people what you're doing. Show a "human face" to the appeal and don't assume that everyone "gets it." Make sure you explain who you are, what the project is, why they should pledge to your project and not someone else's, and when you expect to be finished.

- Keep it short. Under five minutes and preferably under three. Attention spans on the web are measured in seconds, not minutes, so you have to grab them and hook them as fast as possible.

- Make sure your pitch is compelling, but don't try to be smart. A little humility and a dash of humour will go a long way. And make sure the production values are high.

- Include artwork or trailer segments or anything else that helps to sell the idea if you have them, but avoid profanity, blasphemy, or nudity, if you want people to be able to share your video around. Someone may see it and know a friend who will be interested, but if the video is "Not Safe For Work," then they'll think twice about sending out links or embedding it in a blog.

When you start this campaign you also need to know where you audience is going to be hanging out. Start with the kind of film you're making. If it's a science fiction film (of course it is!) then start by approaching the forums and bulletin boards dedicated to the genre, and not just for films either. People who hang out on Sci-Fi book sites also go to the movies, so don't pre-judge who will be interested. Then think about the themes and subject matter involved. If your film is set in a world decimated by climate change, then try to engage environmental and other groups who might be interested. The same is true for groups interested in locations you might use or other speciality things like weapons or costumes. And don't just go steaming in and ask for money. You're seducing them so you need to start a dialogue, get their interest, engage on a personal level first, then make your move. And don't hit and run. Keep visiting, keep them engaged. These people are the audience for your film once it's completed so you need them to stay on-side.

Step 4 — Staying Engaged

Staying engaged is the most important part of your campaign, and while it's pretty straightforward, it does need rigorous attention. You'll need an email list service to thank people and keep them up-to-date with the project. You should have a Twitter account and a Facebook page and Google+ Hangout to drive traffic to your crowdfunding campaign and you'll need a blog and possibly a website to keep the updates rolling. Make full use of those *Like*, *Tweet* and + buttons as well, and encourage everyone involved to help in the word-of-mouth push. Also change your video and update your rewards during the campaign. Statistics show that if you update every five days or so, your pledge rates can double.

A good crowdfunding campaign often starts with your friends and family, and, if you're lucky enough to have one, your existing fan base. By this I mean actual, real friends, not Facebook Friends. People whose mobile numbers and email addresses you have, who you send Christmas cards to and have the occasional beer with. Make a list of those people, and get everyone else involved with the project to make a list as well. It might only come to 50 people, but they are the best 50 people you'll ever start with. Break your campaign up into funding milestones — the beginning, 25% of target, the halfway point, 75% of target and almost there and prod your key contacts to pledge at those milestones. Seeing your campaign push past them can give the casual observer the impetus to also donate. Don't forget to talk to people about the project face to face. It's still the most powerful communications medium there is, so if you get the chance to talk to an audience anywhere about your campaign, then do it.

This is just a brief overview of crowdfunding. It's not meant to be anything more, and if you want more there are in-depth articles online and there are whole books dedicated to the art and craft. What's important to remember, however, is that this is the first real opportunity to test your idea, market your film to an audience, and build support by building a fan base for your film. If you get it right and deliver a great film, you'll also have a solid network upon which to build your next, bigger campaign.

Numerous crowdfunding sites have sprung up dedicated to film, some more popular than others. Here is a list of the most prominent at the time of this printing:

Crowdfunding sites

http://www.kickstarter.com (U.S., UK coming soon)
http://www.indiegogo.com (U.S.)
http://www.buyacredit.com (U.S.)
http://www.piratemyfilm.com/ (U.S.)
https://www.sokap.com/ (Can)
http://www.sponsume.com/ (UK)
http://www.touscoprod.com/ (Fr)
http://www.peopleforcinema.com (Fr)
http://newfacefilm.eu/ (Czech)
http://www.cinecrowd.com (Nl)
http://www.cinemareloaded.com (Nl)
http://www.filminteractor.com (Ger)

Crowdsourcing

Like crowdfunding, crowdsourcing also leverages the power of the Internet to find people, but instead of asking them to donate money, you ask them to donate resources, such as the loan of equipment or access to a particular kind of location, or to donate their time in the shape of skills and experience that can help you bring your film to fruition.

Often you can find people local to where you are who are interested in movies and just want to help out. These people can be drivers, runners, assistants, extras, and so on, but it's also quite possible that, given a small budget to work with, you can find folk with specialist skills that can provide a huge amount of help in areas like costume, props, craft services, painting and decorating, and other more practical tasks.

Then there are the more specialist areas, such as website design and development, online marketing and social media strategy, photography, press kit and PR, and a whole slew of other things that you need to get your film out there, and there are a surprising number of skilled individuals who will work on an interesting project for free, or at cost, because they like the project or want to build a personal portfolio. These people don't even have to be local to you, the nature of the work means that they can be anywhere in the world and you can use the power of the Internet to meet, talk, make decisions, and move forward in tune with your vision. I've also heard of projects where animators, CGI and FX artists, colourists, sound designers, and other major departments within a film production have been outsourced to people in the far corners of the globe because they offered their services and proved they could do the job. As filmmaking becomes more and more democratized, I expect this kind of thing to become more and more common.

Unfortunately, there isn't a one-stop-shop to find these people, it's trial and error and hanging out on the right kind of forums and notice boards that gets it done. But you could start with Shooting People (shootingpeople.org), Talent Circle (talentcircle.org), Mandy (mandy.com), Bullet Film (bulletfilm.com), Filmmaking (filmmaking. net), and Actors and Crew (actorsandcrew.com).

Good luck!

SHOOTING ON DIGITAL

The rise and rise of the DSLR

Over the last few years the entire filmmaking community has embraced DSLR (digital single-lens reflex) cameras like no other digital format before, and the result has been a quantum shift not only in how films are made, but more importantly, who can make them. Improvements in the basic technology along with the huge choice of both new and legacy lenses for DSLRs mean that, cinematically, results are a match for anything film can do, with price points to suit any budget. The proof is out there. Have a browse through any of the online video sites like Vimeo, Daily Motion, Flickr, Vice or Current TV and you can watch thousands of examples of full-resolution HD films, all professionally produced, shot, edited, graded and coloured, but at a fraction of the cost that even a few years ago would have been necessary. DSLRs are light and easy to manoeuvre, especially around actors, allowing for exciting angles and extreme close-ups. They're inconspicuous, looking like ordinary cameras, so you can shoot in the unlikeliest of places without attracting attention. They have excellent low-light capabilities for shooting at night or indoors when it's dark and, what really separates them from video cameras, they allow for very shallow depth-of-field and smooth creamy bokeh that was just not possible on video before DSLRs came along.

But there are trade-offs, of course. Sound on DSLRs has always been an afterthought, so you'll need to shoot professional sound separately on a dedicated device with proper microphones and match it while editing. They are hard to focus, especially at shallow depth-of-field and can be unforgiving of mistakes, and

The future of filmmaking?

with some cameras you have to be careful of problems with pixellation and moire with some backgrounds, and rolling shutter if you move too fast while recording. Their lightness makes them hard to use hand-held without a great deal of shaking, so you'll need a good camera rig to mount your camera onto and a quality tripod. Unfortunately this has the knock-on effect of making you rather more conspicuous, which means that shooting guerilla-style can be a non-starter unless you've planned meticulously for it. Finally, you might find yourself having to get much more technical than you previously ever did. To get the most out of the current crop of DSLRs, especially the micro four-thirds cameras such as the Panasonic Lumix GH2, means hacking the firmware on your camera and tinkering with various internal settings to extract maximum performance. While this means a $700 camera can achieve results that are almost on a par with a RED Epic, it also means learning about B-frames, A-Frames, GOPs, codecs, framerates and much more, not to mention kissing goodbye to your warranty.

But progress cannot be halted and DSLRs are definitely the way forward. A basic DSLR video kit comprises a few items; camera body, two or three lenses, a tripod, a camera rig, a viewfinder or monitor, a sound recorder with one or two microphones, and some fast memory cards. All-in you could be up and running for less than $7,000 new or less than $5,000 if you search around for used stuff, and the beauty of DSLR is that you can update individual items like tripod or microphones as you go. These days, even your investment in camera body and lenses is protected by a huge choice of adapters, increasing their useful life enormously and improving resale value if you do decide to sell them on.

Desktop CGI, Props, And FX

It's inevitable that most of you will crave special effects and CGI on your films no matter how low-budget you've tried to be. And why not; well-executed CGI screams out high production value and even outside of the science fiction genre there's barely any film or TV being shot these days that doesn't have some form of CGI somewhere, even if you don't notice it.

Greenscreen effects are easy to do. I've used a well-lit green curtain as a background before now for simple head and shoulders work and I've also used a corner of a basement with newly plastered walls and a tin of chroma-key paint for full-length shots and both worked perfectly. If you want the best advice on effective greenscreen and bluescreen work check out *GreenScreen Made Easy: Keying and Compositing for Indie Filmmakers* by Jeremy Hanke and Michele Yamazaki. It's the last word on the subject.

There are a number of excellent software packages out there to help you edit your film and composite your special effects, but for a few hundred dollars FXHome makes a whole suite of tools that give you easy lightning, explosions, gunfire, lasers, shockwaves and much more on a home PC. If you want more practical effects like breakaway glass, bloody head shots, a briefcase of prop money, or even a hanged man, then do a web search for Backyard FX and revel in all the terrific video tutorials they have there, for free!

There isn't the space here for me to go into all that could be done by the low-budget filmmaker. That would require a book of its own, and they're out there. But suffice it to say that a little ingenuity and a bit of elbow grease will help you achieve 90% of what you're after and the end results can be every bit as good as a the big boys.

DIGITAL DISTRIBUTION

In the same way the DSLR has revolutionised filmmaking, the Internet has revolutionised distributing your film once it's completed. It's true that a theatrical release is still the thing every filmmaker wants, but with access to film theatres becoming more and more limited and the cost of entering film festivals spiralling ever upwards, it's time to consider using the biggest audience of them all as your bread and butter.

While the use of websites, blogs, and social media as promotional tools for your film are more important than ever, especially if you're trying to sell a hard product like a DVD or a t-shirt, it's as well to remember that online distribution of your film no longer means uploading it for free to YouTube and hoping for some advertising revenue to get your money back. More and more dedicated online distribution companies are springing up every year and you can cut a good deal with the likes of Projector.tv, Distrify, Distribber and even iTunes via iTunes Connect to reach a paying audience for your film.

These guys often have deals with cable and digital TV networks as well as their own online channels so they can tier a package to suit any film and roll it out in different ways using different revenue models. Obviously they will give preference to quality titles that they can have some kind of exclusive rights on, even if it's just for an initial period, but they are in the business of repeat business and as they grow their viewing numbers they need to offer quality entertainment to the audience, entertainment that they cannot get elsewhere. If you can supply it, not just with one film but with a slate of films aimed for production, deals can be had for the enterprising filmmaker.

THE LAST WORD

❧

I dearly hope that you've found this book useful as a guide to writing better science fiction. Hopefully you can recognise the differences between science fiction and fantasy and know the kind of stories that lend themselves well to the genre and why. If everything has gone according to plan, you should also now be equipped to build better worlds, write alien languages, describe alien creatures, and avoid terrible exposition and hoary old science fiction clichés. Mostly though, I hope that with a reasonable grasp of the right kind of science, the audience will really believe what you've written. You might even think about getting out there and making your own film one day, because you no longer need anyone's permission to do so.

But despite my fervent desire that you'll strive to get the science right in your films, always remember that when it comes right down to it, science fiction, as I've said before a few times, is about people. You should write only as much science as is needed, because science fiction is not about technology or spaceships or planets or time travel. It's about plain, ordinary people, like you and me, and the desires and grief and fear and love and revenge and courage and the myriad other emotions that we, the audience, feel and understand as we watch your characters go through their extraordinary story. It's this emotional connective tissue that drives us and binds us all together — even the robots, aliens, and superheroes.

Good luck, and good writing.

Cheers!

Robert Grant

SCIENCE FICTION FILM FESTIVALS

EUROPEAN FESTIVALS

Austria
Slash Film Festival, Wien
http://slashfilmfestival.com

Belgium
Razor Reel Fantastic Film Festival, Brugge
http://www.RRFFF.be

Brussels International Fantastic Film Festival, Brussels
http://www.festivalfantastique.org/festival

Croatia
Fantastic Zagreb Film Festival, Zagreb
http://www.fantastic-zagreb.com

Estonia
Haapsalu Horror & Fantasy Film Festival, Happsalu
http://www.hoff.ee

Black Nights Film Festival, Tallinn
http://www.poff.ee

Finland
Espoo Ciné International Film Festival, Espoo
http://www.espoocine.fi

France
Festival de Cannes, Cannes
http://www.festival-cannes.com

Le Festival International du Film Fantastique de Gérardmer, Gérardmer
http://www.festival-gerardmer.com

Hallucinations Collectives Film Festival, Lyon
http://www.hallucinations-collectives.com

Utopiales — Festival International de Science-Fiction de Nantes, Nantes
http://www.utopiales.org

Fantastique Semaine du Cinéma, Nice
http://www.cinenasty.com

Festival International Du Film Merveilleux, Paris
http://www.festival-film-merveilleux.com

G.E.N.R.E., Paris
http://genrefestival.com

Paris International Fantastic Film Festival, Paris
http://www.pifff.fr

Strasbourg European Fantastic Film Festival, Strasbourg
http://www.spectrefilm.com

Germany
Fantasy Film Nights, Berlin
http://www.fantasyfilmfest.com

Weekend of Fear Film Festival, Erlangen
http://www.weekend-of-fear.de

Greece
Athens International Sci-Fi & Fantasy Film Festival, Athens
http://sffrated.wordpress.com

Screamin Athens Horror Film Festival, Athens
http://sahff.blogspot.com

Italy
Ravenna Nightmare Film Festival, Ravenna
http://www.ravennanightmare.it

Fanta Festival, Roma
http://www.fanta-festival.it

Trieste International Science Fiction Film Festival, Trieste
http://www.scienceplusfiction.org

TOHorror Film Festival, Turin
http://www.tohorrorfilmfest.it

Ireland
The Golden Blasters Film Festival, Dublin
http://www.octocon.com/goldenblasters

Horrorthon Film Festival, Dublin
http://www.horrorthon.com

Latvia
Riga International Fantasy Film Festival, Riga
http://www.arsenals.lv

The Netherlands
IMAGINE: Amsterdam Fantastic Film Festival, Amsterdam
http://www.imaginefilmfestival.nl

Poland
Sopot Film Festival, Sopot
http://www.sopotfilmfestival.pl

Portugal
MOTELx, Lisbon
http://www.motelx.org

Slovenia
Grossmann Fantastic Film & Wine Festival, Ljutomer
http://www.grossmann.si

Spain
CryptShow Festival, Barcelona
http://www.cryptshow.com

FanCine Málaga — Festival de Cine Fantástico, Malaga
http://www.fancine.org

FANT, Fantasy Film Festival, Bilbao
http://www.fantbilbao.net

San Sebastian Horror and Fantasy Film Festival, San Sebastian
http://www.donostiakultura.com/terror/2010/en/index.php

Sitges — Festival Internacional de Cinema de Catalunya, Sitges
http://sitgesfilmfestival.com

Sweden
Lund International Fantastic Film Festival, Lund
http://www.fff.se

Switzerland
Neuchâtel International Fantastic Film Festival, Neuchâtel
http://www.nifff.ch

United Kingdom
Abertoir Horror Festival, Aberystwyth
http://www.abertoir.co.uk

Dead by Dawn Horror Film Festival, Edinburgh
http://www.deadbydawn.co.uk

Leeds International Film Festival: Fanomenon, Leeds
http://www.leedsfilm.com

FrightFest, London
http://www.frightfest.co.uk

London Horror Film Festival, London
http://www.londonhorrorfestival.com

SCI-FI-LONDON: London International Festival of Science Fiction and Fantastic Film, London
http://www.sci-fi-london.com

Grimm Up North!, Manchester
http://www.grimmfest.com

Mayhem Horror Fest, Nottingham
http://www.mayhemhorrorfest.co.uk

Celluloid Screams: Sheffield Horror Film Festival, Sheffield
http://www.celluloidscreams.co.uk

Bram Stoker International Film Festival, Whitby
http://bramstokerfilmfestival.com

NORTH AMERICAN FILM FESTIVALS

USA

Arizona
Phoenix Fear Film Festival, Phoenix
http://phxfearfilmfestival.com

International Horror & Sci-Fi Film Festival, Scottsdale
http://www.horrorscifi.com

California
Big Bear Horror-Fi Film Festival, Big Bear Lake
http://bigbearhorrorfilmfest.com

Burbank International Film Festival, Burbank
http://www.burbankfilmfestival.org

ShockFest Film Festival, Hollywood
http://www.shockfilmfest.com

BleedFest Film Festival, Los Angeles
http://www.bleedfest.com

Famous Monsters of Filmland: Imagi-Movies Film Festival, Los Angeles
http://www.imagimovies.com

Midnight Black International Film Festival, Los Angeles
http://www.midnightblackinternational.com

Screamfest LA, Los Angeles
http://www.screamfestla.com

Shriekfest, Los Angeles
http://www.shriekfest.com

Viscera Film Festival, Los Angeles
http://www.viscerafilmfestival.com

ZedFest, North Hollywood
http://zedfest.org

Everybody Dies Film Festival, Orange County
http://www.everybodydiesfilmfest.com

Action On Film Festival, Pasadena
http://www.aoffest.com

Shockerfest, Riverside
http://www.shockerfest.com

Comic-Con International Independent Film Festival, San Diego
http://www.comic-con.org/cci/cci_iff.php

Horrible Imaginings Film Festival, San Diego
http://www.horribleimaginingsfilmfest.com

Another Hole in the Head, San Francisco
http://www.sfindie.com

Tabloid Witch Awards, Santa Monica
http://www.taboidwitch.com

H.P. Lovecraft Film Festival, San Pedro
http://www.hplfilmfestival.com

Colorado
Mile High Horror Film Festival, Denver
http://www.milehighhorrorfestival.com

Telluride Horror Show, Telluride
http://www.telluridehorrorshow.com

Florida
Geek Film Festival, Miami
http://www.geekfilmfest.com

Freak Show Horror Film Festival, Orlando
http://www.freakshowfilmfest.com

Georgia
Buried Alive Film Fest, Atlanta
http://buriedalivefilmfest.com

Dragon*Con Film Festival, Atlanta
http://filmfest.dragoncon.org

HorrorQuest Film Festival, Atlanta
http://www.thehorrorquest.com

Illinois
Chicago Horror Film Festival, Chicago
http://chicagohorrorfest.com

Indy Horror Film Festival, Dekalb
http://www.indyhorrorfilmfest.com

B-Fest, Evanston
http://www.b-fest.com

Drunken Zombie Film Festival, Peoria
http://drunkenzombiefilmfestival.com

Indiana
Dark Carnival Film Festival, Bloomington
http://darkcarnivalfilmfest.com

B Movie Celebration, Franklin
http://www.bmoviecelebration.com

GenCon International Film Festival, Indianapolis
http://www.gencon.com

Kentucky
Fright Night Film Festival, Louisville
http://frightnightfilmfest.com

Louisiana
Fear Fete Horror Film Festival, New Orleans
http://www.fearfete.com

New Orleans Horror Film Festival, New Orleans
http://neworleanshorrorfilmfestival.com

Vampire Film Festival, New Orleans
http://www.vampirefilmfestival.com

Massachusetts
Boston Sci-Fi, Boston
http://scifi.vintagelinux.com

Boston Underground Film Festival, Boston
http://www.bostonunderground.org

Killer Film Fest, Somerville
http://www.killerfilmfest.com

Michigan
Thriller! Chiller!, Grand Rapids
http://www.thrillerchiller.com

Kalamazoo Horror Fest, Kalamazoo
http://www.kzoohorrorfest.com

New York
Doomsday Film Festival, Brookyln
http://doomsdayfilmfest.com

The Science of Horror Film Festival, Brooklyn
http://dedpro.com/horror

Buffalo Screams Horror Film Festival, Buffalo
http://buffaloscreams.com

New York Asian Film Festival, New York
http://www.subwaycinema.com

Royal Flush Festival, New York
http://www.royalflushfestival.com

Tribeca Film Festival: Midnight, New York
http://www.tribecafilm.com/festival

Tromadance Film Festival, New York
http://www.tromadance.com

North Carolina
ActionFest, Asheville
http://actionfest.com

Nevermore Film Festival, Durham
http://festivals.carolinatheatre.org/nevermore

Corpsedance International Horror Film Festival, Raleigh
http://www.corpsedanceihff.com

Nevada
Renovation Independent/Fan Film Festival, Reno
http://www.renovationsf.org/filmfest.php

Oklahoma
Tulsa International Film Festival: Nightmare Division, Tulsa
http://www.tulsafilmfestival.org

Ohio
Ohio 24 Hour Horror Marathon, Columbus
http://www.scifimarathon.com/horror

Ohio 24 Hour Science Fiction Marathon, Columbus
http://www.scifimarathon.com

Oregon
Grindhouse Film Festival, Portland
http://www.grindhousefilmfest.com

Pennsylvania
Eerie Horror Film Festival, Eerie
http://www.eeriehorrorfest.com

Philadelphia Cinefest! Danger After Dark, Philadelphia
http://www.dangerafterdark.com

QFest! Danger After Dark, Philadelphia
http://www.dangerafterdark.com

Terror Film Festival, Philadelphia
http://terrorfilmfestival.net

Pittsburgh Horror Film Festival, Pittsburgh
http://pittsburghhorrorfilms.com

Rhode Island
Rhode Island International Horror Film Festival, Providence
http://www.film-festival.org/HorrorCALENDAR11.php

Texas
Fantastic Fest, Austin
http://www.fantasticfest.com

San Antonio Horrific Film Fest, San Antonio
http://www.horrificfilmfest.com

SXSW Midnighters & SXFantastic, Austin
http://sxsw.com

Tennessee
Knoxville Horror Film Festival, Knoxville
http://www.knoxvillehorrorfest.com

Utah
Salty Horror International Film Festival, Salt Lake City
http://www.tshiff.com

Washington D.C.
Spooky Movie — The Washington, D.C. International Horror Film Festival, Washington, D.C.
http://www.spookyfests.com

Washington State
Science Fiction + Fantasy Short Film Festival, Seattle
http://www.empsfm.org/filmfestival

Seattle International Film Festival: Midnight Adrenaline, Seattle
http://www.siff.net

Maelstrom International Fantastic Film Festival, Seattle
http://www.mifff.org

Tri-City Independent/Fan Film Festival, Tri-Cities
http://www.tcif3.com

CANADA

Alberta
Calgary Underground Film Festival, Calgary
http://www.calgaryundergroundfilm.org

British Columbia
B-Grade Horrorfest, Whistler
http://www.heavyhitting.com

Ontario
Toronto After Dark Film Festival, Toronto
http://torontoafterdark.com

Toronto International Film Festival: Midnight Madness, Toronto
http://tiff.net

Quebec
Fantastia Festival, Montreal
http://www.fantasiafestival.com

Saskatchewan
Dark Bridges Film Festival, Saskatoon
http://www.darkbridges.com

SOUTH AMERICAN FILM FESTIVALS

Argentina
Buenos Aires Rojo,Sangre Buenos Aires
http://rojosangre.quintadimension.com

Brazil
Mostra Goiana De Filmes Independentes, Goiania City
http://www.mostratrash.com.br

Fantaspoa — International Fantastic Film Festival of Porto Alegre,
Porto Alegre
http://www.fantaspoa.com

AnimaCursed, Rio de Janeiro
http://www.animaldicoados.com

RIO Fan, Rio de Janeiro
http://www.riofan.com.br

Cinefantasy, São Paulo
http://www.cinefantastico.com.br

Chile
FIXION-SARS, Festival de Cine Fantástico y de Terror de Santiago,
Santiago
http://www.fixionsars.com

Mexico
Post Mortem Fest, Aguascalientes
http://www.postmortemfest.com

Aurora: Muestra de Cine de Horror, Guanajuato
htpp://www.aurorahorror.com

MACABRO Mexico City International Horror Film Festival,
Mexico City
http://www.macabro.mx

Morbido Film Festival, Mexico City
http://www.morbidofest.com

Puerto Rico
Puerto Rico Horror Film Festival, Guaynabo
http://www.horrorpr.com

Uruguay
Montevideo Fantastico, Calonnes
http://www.montevideofantastico.com.uy

AFRICA/ASIA-PACIFIC FILM FESTIVALS

Australia
Bloodfest Fantastique Film Festival, Melbourne
http://www.bloodfest.com.au

Fantastic Asia Film Festival, Melbourne
http://faff.com.au

Hello Darkness Film Festival, Melbourne
http://www.hellodarkness.com.au

A Night of Horror International Film Festival, Sydney
http://www.anightofhorror.com

Fantastic Planet: Sydney Science Fiction & Fantasy Film Festival, Sydney
http://www.fantasticplanetfilmfestival.com

Cape Town
Celludroid Film Festival, Cape Town
http://www.celludroid.net

South African HorrorFest, Cape Town
http://www.horrorfest.info

The X Fest, Cape Town
http://www.xfest.org

Israel
Icon Fantastic Film Festival, Tel-Aviv
http://www.icon.org.il/2010

Indonesia
Indonesia International Fantastic Film Festival, Jakarta
http://www.inafff.com

Japan
Yubari International Fantastic Film Festival, Yubari
http://yubarifanta.com

New Zealand
New Zealand International Film Festival Incredible Strange, Auckland
http://www.nzff.co.nz

South Korea
Busan International Film Festival: Midnight Passion, Busan
http://www.biff.kr

Korean International Science Fiction Film Festival, Gwacheon
http://www.gisf.org

Puchon International Fantastic Film Festival, Puchon
http://www.pifan.com

Mise-en-scène Short Film Festival, Seoul
http://www.msff.or.kr

Taiwan
Golden Horse Fantastic Film Festival, Taipei
http://www.ghfff.org.tw

A SELECTED SCIENCE FICTION TIMELINE

❧

(FICTION)

While you can probably trace science fiction writing back to the *Epic of Gilgamesh* around 3,000 years ago, it more likely started to surface in the 1600s with Johannes Kepler's *Somnium* and Cyrano de Bergerac's *The Other World*. It continued to blossom in the 1700s with works by Jonathan Swift and Daniel Defoe, amongst others, and then exploded in the Victorian 1800s and hasn't really stopped since. There isn't close to enough room to mention everything published over the last century of science fiction writing, especially given the huge output of the 1950s and '60s, but as the influences and source material for many motion pictures are plain to see, I have picked out a few personal favourites.

1818 — Mary Shelley publishes *Frankenstein, or The Modern Prometheus*. Generally regarded as the first proper science fiction novel.

1865 — Jules Verne publishes *Journey to the Centre of the Earth*.

1869 — Edward Everett Hale publishes *The Brick Moon*. First ever mention of a satellite orbiting the Earth.

1870 — Jules Verne publishes *20,000 Leagues Under The Sea*.

1886 — Robert Louis Stevenson publishes *The Strange Case of Dr. Jekyll and Mr. Hyde*.

1889 — Mark Twain publishes *A Connecticut Yankee in King Arthur's Court*.

1895 — H.G. Wells publishes *The Time Machine*.

1898 — H.G. Wells publishes *The War of the Worlds*.

1909 — E.M. Forster publishes *The Machine Stops*.

1910 — P.G. Wodehouse publishes *The Swoop*. Probably the first spoofing of the science fiction genre.

1917 — Edgar Rice Burroughs publishes *A Princess of Mars*. First of the hugely influential 'Barsoom' series

1923 — Karel Capek publishes *R.U.R. Rossum's Universal Robots*. First recorded use of the word "robot" in science fiction.

1924 — Yevgeny Zamiatin publishes *We* and becomes first Russian dissident.

1925 — Hugo Gernsback (for whom the famous award is named) publishes *Ralph 124C41+: A Romance of the Year 2660*.

1926 — *Amazing Stories* magazine first published. The first magazine that published exclusively science fiction.

1930 — Olaf Stapledon publishes *Last and First Men*.

1932 — Aldous Huxley publishes *Brave New World*.

1936 — Olaf Stapledon publishes *Star Maker*. The most influential novel from one of science fiction's most influential writers.

1949 — George Orwell publishes *Nineteen Eighty-Four*. George R. Stewart publishes *Earth Abides*.

1950 — Isaac Asimov publishes *I, Robot*. Ray Bradbury publishes *The Martian Chronicles*. Fifteen science fiction magazines begin publication including *Galaxy*, *Worlds Beyond*, and *Science Fiction*.

1951 — Isaac Asimov publishes *Foundation*. Ray Bradbury publishes *The Illustrated Man*. John Wyndham publishes *The Day of the Triffids*. Arthur C. Clarke publishes *Prelude to Space*. First mention of communications satellites (based on his own invention).

1952 — Philip Jose Farmer publishes *The Lovers*. First, and shocking, mention of a sexual relationship between a human and an alien.

1953 — The first annual Hugo Award named after Hugo Gernsback is given. Ray Bradbury publishes *Fahrenheit 451*.

1955 — Jack Finney publishes *The Body Snatchers* (later adapted for into *Invasion of the Body Snatchers*).

1959 — Robert A. Heinlein publishes *Starship Troopers*.

1960 — Walter M. Miller Jr. publishes *A Canticle for Leibowitz*. *Analog* magazine begins publication.

1961 — Robert A. Heinlein publishes *Stranger in a Strange Land*. Tech nerds might be interested to know this is where the term "grok" comes from. Stanislaw Lem publishes Solaris.

1962 — Philip K. Dick publishes *The Man in the High Castle*. Probably still the most adapted science fiction author of all time, his work continues to be adapted and re-made to this day. Anthony Burgess publishes *A Clockwork Orange*. Richard Condon publishes *The Manchurian Candidate*. J.G. Ballard publishes *The Drowned World*.

1965 — Frank Herbert publishes *Dune*.

1968 — Philip K. Dick publishes *Do Androids Dream of Electric Sheep*. Arthur C. Clarke publishes *2001: A Space Odyssey*. Kurt Vonnegut publishes *Slaughterhouse Five*.

1969 — Ursula K. Le Guin publishes *The Left Hand of Darkness*, a controversial novel about gender often referred to as the first feminist science fiction. Michael Crichton publishes *The Andromeda Strain*.

1976 — Frank Herbert publishes *Children of Dune*. After it sold 100,000 copies, publishers figured out science fiction was big business.

1977 — Philip K. Dick publishes *A Scanner Darkly*.

1978 — Paddy Chayefsky publishes *Altered States*.

1978 — *Omni* magazine begins publication.

1979 — Stephen King publishes *The Dead Zone*. Interestingly a World Fantasy Award finalist, but King withdrew it from the ballot so it would be seen as a science fiction novel and not a fantasy.

1979 — Douglas Adams publishes *The Hitchhiker's Guide to the Galaxy* (novel).

1980 — Arthur C. Clarke publishes *The Fountains of Paradise*. First mention of the "skyhook" a space-elevator, linked from earth to a geosynchronous space station.

1984 — William Gibson publishes *Neuromancer*.

1985 — Orson Scott Card publishes *Ender's Game*.

1987 — Iain M. Banks publishes *Consider Phlebas*. The first of The Culture novels.

1990 — William Gibson & Bruce Sterling publish *The Difference Engine*.

1992 — Neal Stephenson publishes *Snowcrash*.

1993 — Kim Stanley Robinson publishes *Red Mars*.

1994 — Pat Cadigan publishes *Fools*.

2001 — China Miéville publishes *Perdido Street Station*. Jasper Fforde publishes *The Eyre Affair*.

2002 — Neil Gaiman publishes *American Gods*. Carol Emshwiller publishes *The Mount*.

2003 — Cory Doctorow publishes *Down and Out in the Magic Kingdom*. The first novel released under a Creative Commons licence. Charles Stross publishes *Singularity Sky*. Audrey Niffenegger publishes *The Time Traveler's Wife*. Neal Stephenson publishes *Quicksilver*, Book 1 of The Baroque Cycle. Margaret Atwood publishes *Oryx and Crake*. William Gibson publishes *Pattern Recognition*.

2004 — Andrew Sean Greer publishes *The Confessions of Max Tivoli*.

2005 — Geoff Ryman publishes *Air: Or, Have not Have*.

2006 — Charles Stross publishes *Glasshouse*.

2007 — Ken MacLeod publishes *The Execution Channel*.

2008 — Ekaterina Sedia publishes *The Alchemy of Stone*. Nick Harkaway publishes *The Gone-Away World*.

2009 — Paolo Bacigalupi publishes *The Windup Girl*.

2010 — Ian McDonald publishes *The Dervish House*.

2011 — Jane Rogers publishes *The Testament of Jessie Lamb*.

A Selected Science Fiction Timeline

~

(Film)

Considering that there are more than a hundred years of science fiction films in this list, covering every kind of scientific, technological, social and cultural event in every setting and across every world stage imaginable, there's pretty much something for everyone here. Go ahead and check for your favourites, but make notes of those you haven't seen and be sure to check them out. Especially if you've only ever seen the remakes, check out the originals and see which you prefer.

1902 — Georges Méliès, considered the "Grandfather of Special Effects," makes *Le Voyage dans la Lune* (A Trip To The Moon). Possibly the first science fiction film ever made.

1910 — Thomas Edison makes the first film version of *Frankenstein*.

1913 — *Dr. Jekyll and Mr. Hyde*

1916 — *20,000 Leagues Under the Sea*

1924 — *Aelita: Queen of Mars* becomes the first Soviet science fiction film.

1925 — Sir Arthur Conan Doyle's novel *The Lost World* is adapted by First National Pictures with pioneering stop motion effects by Willis O'Brien.

1927 — *Metropolis*

1930 — Science fiction musical-comedy *Just Imagine* released. It's a huge flop.

1931 — *Frankenstein*. Possibly the first remake.

1933 — *The Invisible Man*

1936 — *Flash Gordon*

1937 — *Lost Horizon*

1938 — *Buck Rogers*

1948 — *Abbott and Costello Meet Frankenstein, Superman*

1951 — *The Day the Earth Stood Still*

1953 — *The War of the Worlds*

1954 — *20,000 Leagues under the Sea, Them!, Godzilla*

1955 — *This Island Earth*

1956 — *Invasion of the Body Snatchers, Forbidden Planet, 1984*

1959 — *Plan 9 From Outer Space*

1960 — *The Time Machine, The Lost World*

1962 — *The Manchurian Candidate*

1963 — *The Birds, Children of the Damned, The Man with the X-Ray Eyes*

1966 — *Fantastic Voyage, Fahrenheit 451*

1968 — *2001: A Space Odyssey, Planet of the Apes*

1971 — *A Clockwork Orange, The Andromeda Strain, THX 1138, The Omega Man*

1972 — *Solaris*

1973 — *Sleeper, Soylent Green, Westworld*

1974 — *Dark Star, The Stepford Wives*

1975 — *Rollerball, Death Race 2000*

1976 — *The Man Who Fell to Earth, Logan's Run*

1977 — *Star Wars, Close Encounters of the Third Kind, Eraserhead*

A Selected Science Fiction Timeline (Film)

1978 — *Invasion of the Body Snatchers, The Boys from Brazil, Superman, Capricorn One*

1979 — *Alien, Mad Max, Buck Rogers in the 25th Century, Stalker, Star Trek The Motion Picture, Moonraker*

1980 — *Altered States, The Empire Strikes Back*

1981 — *Outland, Escape from New York, Time Bandits, Quest for Fire, Mad Max 2*

1982 — *Blade Runner, E.T.: The Extra-Terrestrial, Star Trek The Wrath of Khan, Tron, The Thing*

1983 — *WarGames, Videodrome, Brainstorm*

1984 — *The Dead Zone, Return of the Jedi, The Man with Two Brains, Dune, 1984, The Philadelphia Experiment, Runaway*

1985 — *Cocoon, Brazil, Mad Max Beyond Thunderdome, Explorers, Back to the Future, Enemy Mine, The Quiet Earth*

1986 — *The Fly, When the Wind Blows, Aliens*

1987 — *Akira, Predator, The Running Man, Robocop*

1989 — *Bill and Ted's Excellent Adventure, Batman, Back to the Future II*

1990 — *Flatliners, The Handmaid's Tale, Total Recall, Back to the Future III*

1991 — *Terminator 2 Judgment Day, The Rocketeer*

1993 — *Jurassic Park*

1994 — *Stargate, Mary Shelley's Frankenstein*

1995 — *Twelve Monkeys, Outbreak, Tank Girl, Johnny Mnemonic, Judge Dread, Species, Waterworld, Strange Days, The City of Lost Children, Ghost in the Shell*

1996 — *Independence Day, Space Jam, Mars Attacks*

1997 — *The Fifth Element, Men in Black, Contact, Event Horizon, Mimic, Gattaca, Starship Troopers*

215

1998 — *The Truman Show, Pi, Dark City, Deep Impact, Godzilla, Armageddon, Small Soldiers*

1999 — *The Matrix, The Iron Giant, Galaxy Quest, eXistenZ, Star Wars: Episode I — The Phantom Menace*

2000 — *Pitch Black, X-Men*

2001 — *Donnie Darko, The American Astronaut, Ever Since the World Ended, A.I. Artificial Intelligence, Final Fantasy: The Spirits Within, K-Pax*

2002 — *Cypher, 28 Days Later, Minority Report, Resident Evil, Equilibrium*

2003 — *Paycheck, Robot Stories, Code 46*

2004 — *The Incredibles, Primer, Eternal Sunshine of the Spotless Mind*

2005 — *The Island, Serenity, War of the Worlds, Fantastic Four*

2006 — *Children of Men, Cloverfield, V for Vendetta*

2007 — *Next, Sunshine, Transformers, 28 Weeks Later, I Am Legend*

2008 — *The Incredible Hulk, Iron Man, Hancock, Wall-E*

2009 — *Avatar, The Road, Eyeborgs, Moon, District 9, Splice*

2010 — *Inception, TRON: Legacy, Radio Free Albemuth, Hot Tub Time Machine, Monsters*

2011 — *Super 8, PIG, Attack the Block, Rise of the Planet of the Apes, Source Code, Limitless, Paul, Captain America: The First Avenger, The Adjustment Bureau, Cowboys & Aliens, Hugo, Thor*

2012 — *The Hunger Games, Battleship, John Carter, The Avengers*

A Selected Science Fiction Timeline

❧

(Television)

This list is not a full account of all science fiction found on television, but it does include some important and popular shows. If anything is to be learned from it, it's this; science fiction has always proved to be popular on TV and science fiction shows seem to make up a bigger proportion of shows every year. If you hit the zeitgeist your following can be huge and vocal with the ability to run and run and the likelihood of a remake is good. Unless you're on Fox.

1949 — *Captain Video and his Video Rangers* (DuMont Television Network)

1950 — *Buck Rogers* (ABC)

1953 — *Flash Gordon* (Intercontinental Television Films/ Interwest Films (West Germany)/Telediffusion (France), *The Quatermass Experiment* (BBC)

1955 — *Science Fiction Theatre* (Ivan Tors Productions)

1959 — *The Twilight Zone* (CBS), *The Adventures of Superman* (ABC)

1961 — *A for Andromeda* (BBC)

1962 — *The Jetsons* (Hanna-Barbera), *Fireball XL5* (ITC Entertainment)

1963 — *The Outer Limits* (ABC), *My Favorite Martian* (CBS), *Dr. Who* (BBC, and still going strong!)

1964 — *Voyage to the Bottom of the Sea* (ABC)

1965 — *Lost in Space* (CBS), *Thunderbirds* (ITC Entertainment)

1966 — *The Time Tunnel* (Irwin Allen Productions), *Star Trek* (NBC)

1967 — *The Invaders* (ABC)

1968 — *Land of the Giants* (Irwin Allen Productions), *The Prisoner* (ITC Entertainment)

1970 — *UFO* (ITC Entertainment)

1973 — *The Six Million Dollar Man* (ABC), *The Tomorrow People* (ITV)

1974 — *Wonder Woman* (ABC/CBS), *Planet of the Apes* (CBS), *Space: 1999* (ITC Entertainment. At the time the highest ever budget for a science fiction TV series)

1975 — *Survivors* (BBC)

1976 — *The Bionic Woman* (ABC)

1978 — *Mork & Mindy* (ABC), *Battlestar Galactica* (ABC), *Blake's 7* (BBC)

1979 — *Buck Rogers in the 25th Century* (NBC)

1980 — *The Martian Chronicles* (NBC)

1981 — *The Hitchhiker's Guide to the Galaxy* (BBC)

1983 — *V* (NBC)

1985 — *Steven Spielberg's Amazing Stories* (NBC), *Max Headroom* (Channel 4)

1986 — *ALF* (NBC)

1987 — *Star Trek: The Next Generation* (CBS)

1988 — *Mystery Science Theater 3000* (Best Brains), *Red Dwarf* (BBC)

1989 — *Alien Nation* (Fox), *Quantum Leap* (NBC)

1993 — *Star Trek: Deep Space Nine* (CBS), *The X-Files* (Fox)

1994 — *Babylon 5* (Warner TV), *RoboCop: The Series* (Fox), *Earth 2* (NBC)

1995 — *ReBoot* (Mainframe Entertainment. First all computer-animated TV series), *Sliders* (Fox), *Space: Above and Beyond* (Fox — still one of my favourite TV shows!)

1996 – *3rd Rock From The Sun* (NBC)

1999 — *Futurama* (Fox), *Farscape* (Nine Network)

2000 — *Dark Angel* (Fox)

2002 — *Firefly* (Fox — should never have been cancelled!)

2004 — *Lost* (ABC), *Battlestar Galactica* (Sci-Fi Channel), *The 4400* (Paramount)

2005 — *Dr. Who* (BBC)

2006 — *A Town Called Eureka* (SyFy), *Heroes* (NBC)

2008 — *Fringe* (Fox), *Terminator: The Sarah Connor Chronicles* (Fox), *Sanctuary* (SyFy)

2009 — *Misfits* (E4), *Warehouse 13* (SyFy), *Dollhouse* (Fox), *V* (Warner TV)

2010 — *The Walking Dead* (AMC), *Haven* (SyFy)

2011 — *Terra Nova* (Fox), *Alphas* (SyFy), *Falling Skies* (Dreamworks/TNT)

2012 — *Alcatraz* (Fox), *Revolution* (NBC)

REFERENCED FILMS

The author acknowledges the copyright owners of the following motion pictures and TV shows from which single frames have been used in this book for purposes of commentary, criticism and scholarship under the Fair Use Doctrine.

A Clockwork Orange ©1977 Warner Bros. Pictures, All Rights Reserved.

A Sound of Thunder ©2005 Warner Bros. Pictures, All Rights Reserved.

Attack the Block ©2011 Studio Canal Features, All Rights Reserved.

Avatar ©2009 Twentieth Century Fox, All Rights Reserved.

Back to the Future ©1985 Universal Pictures, All Rights Reserved.

Bicentennial Man ©1999 1492 Pictures, All Rights Reserved.

Blade Runner ©1982 Warner Bros. Pictures, All Rights Reserved.

Brazil ©1985 Universal Pictures, All Rights Reserved.

Contact ©1997 Warner Bros. Pictures, All Rights Reserved.

Defying Gravity ©2009 Twentieth Century Fox, All Rights Reserved.

District 9 ©2009 Tri-Star Pictures, All Rights Reserved.

Fringe ©2008 Warner Bros. Television, All Rights Reserved.

Hancock ©2008 Columbia Pictures, All Rights Reserved.

I, Robot ©2004 Twentieth Century Fox, All Rights Reserved.

Inception ©2010 Warner Bros. Pictures, All Rights Reserved.

Independence Day ©1996 Twentieth Century Fox, All Rights Reserved.

It Happened Here ©1966 Rath Films, All Rights Reserved.

John Carter ©2012 Walt Disney Pictures, All Rights Reserved.

Johnny Mnemonic ©1995 Tri-Star Pictures, All Rights Reserved.

GLOSSARY

~

Agent: An autonomous entity, usually based in software, that can be set upon a continuing course of action. This could be by scouring a network for specific types of data or information and producing collated results for a user, or it could be through sensors or other means to monitor and control an environment. Agents can be very simple, acting alone for a single purpose, or very complex, acting in concert with many other agents to achieve their purpose.

AI (Artificial Intelligence): A machine, computer, intelligent agent or system, designed by humans, that has the ability to perceive its own environment and take actions to protect itself, and effect diagnostics and repairs upon itself, in order to thrive within that confine.

Alcubierre Drive: A mathematically possible idea, proposed by Miguel Alcubierre and based on a solution of Einstein's field equations, by which a spacecraft could achieve FTL travel. Because it is impossible for an object to accelerate to the speed of light, if the space around it had negative mass and could somehow be contracted at the front and expanded to the rear, travel would effectively be faster than light.

Alien: A life form not indigenous to Earth and assumed to be extra-terrestrial in origin or an artefact, behaviour, or action that is foreign to Earth or to humans in composition, nature, or derivation.

Alternate History: A story set on a version of Earth where history has diverged from our own actual history, resulting in a significantly different social and/or political culture.

Alternate Reality: *See* Alternate History

Alternate World: A world — possibly a version of our own Earth, but not necessarily — that has a different social/cultural/political make-up, and/or a different set of physical laws, than that of our own world.

Android: A type of robot, usually containing biological parts or elements, that is designed to closely mimic the look, and often feel, of a human.

Ansible: A word coined by author Ursula K. Le Guin that means a device capable of instantaneous communication (with a similar device) over any distance with zero lag or delay time.

Anti-gravity: A hypothetical technology that can nullify the effects of gravity on an object or within a particular place, allowing (usually large and heavy) things to be moved or transported with relative ease. It is rarely clear how the technology works, but it is assumed that the effects of gravity are balanced-out by electromagnets or some similar force.

Antimatter: A term derived from particle physics, antimatter is material composed of antiparticles which have bonded together in the same way that normal particles bind to form normal matter. In science fiction terms, because antiparticles possess opposite charge and quantum spin to ordinary particles, mixing matter and antimatter together can lead to the annihilation of both, usually in a massive release of explosive energy.

Artificial Environment: An environment that has been designed and built for the benefit of its inhabitants, for example a bio-dome or greenhouse for the growing of crops where the natural environment would not support their growth.

Artificial Human: *See* Android

Artificial Life (A-Life): In sci-fi terms this means the creation of living, sentient creatures by humans and covers everything from *Frankenstein* to *I Robot*. In real terms it means the computer modelling of complex, life-like behaviour. Artificial Life forms have the ability to evolve beyond the confines of the rules programmed into them and exhibit their own learned behaviour.

Artificial Person: *See* Android

Assembler: A machine or system of nanomachines that can be programmed to build virtually any molecular structure or device from its constituent chemical building blocks, analogous to sculpting a plastic part using a 3D printer.

Asimov's Three Laws of Robotics: A set of rules devised by the author Isaac Asimov as a safety feature which cannot be bypassed. The Three Laws are:

- A robot may not injure a human being or, through inaction, allow a human being to come to harm.
- A robot must obey the orders given to it by human beings, except where such orders would conflict with the First Law.
- A robot must protect its own existence as long as such protection does not conflict with the First or Second Laws.

As you might expect, many of Asimov's robot stories involve robots behaving in ways that are counter to the Three Laws.

Augment: To enhance and expand a person's physical or cognitive abilities beyond the range of natural humans using technologically.

Autoevolution: Evolution directed by intelligent beings instead of natural selection.

Automated Engineering: A specialised form of artificial intelligence where computers perform engineering design and manufacture, evolving and refining the design, despite only broad outline specifications provided by humans.

Baby Universe: A small, artificially created universe, linked to its old or parent universe by a wormhole, and which could theoretically be used for additional living space, massive computing, or as an escape from a dying parent universe.

Beam Down/Beam Up: From *Star Trek*, the transporting of someone from ship to planet or vice versa by disintegrating them at a molecular level, sending the molecules to their destination using a light beam, and then re-integrating them upon arrival.

Beanstalk: A huge cable tethered to the Earth at one end and to a geosynchronous satellite at the other in order to provide easy and cheap access to space using elevators.

Bernal Sphere: A type of space habitat designed for colonisation and intended as a long-term home for permanent residents.

Berserker: A self-replicating, self-repairing machine that has been programmed to destroy all life in its path.

Big Bang: The theory that, approximately 13.75 billion years ago, the Universe was in an extremely hot, dense state, and expanded rapidly, causing it to cool, which resulted in its present continuously expanding state.

Big Crunch: The opposite of the Big Bang, is the singularity at the end of time, in a collapsing universe.

Bionics: Popularised by *The Six Million Dollar Man*, bionics is the science of connecting artificial organs or limbs to existing biological systems to produce augmented humans.

Biostasis: Suspension of all biological activity in a human patient by infusing them with cryoprotective chemicals and freezing or vitrifying them.

B-Life: Biological Life (as opposed to A-Life).

Blind (or Brute Force) Uploading: Uploading of somebody by scanning and directly simulating their neural patterns without adaptation or refinement.

Biotechnology: A theoretical branch of science that combines technologies like genetic engineering, nanotechnology, surgical construction, and bionics in order to augment, enhance, and manipulate living tissue with the ease and degree of sophistication that we can currently apply to non-living things.

Black Hole: A black hole is an area in space formed when a massive star collapses at the end of its life, and from which gravity prevents anything from escaping. Surrounding a black hole there is a boundary known as the Event Horizon, through which matter and light can only pass inward, towards the mass of the black hole. Nothing can escape a black hole once beyond the event horizon, but a black hole can continue to grow by absorbing mass from its surroundings.

Blaster: First coined in the 1930s, it's a catch-all term that refers to a handheld weapon, similar to a handgun, but firing some form of ray or energy pulse.

Chrononauts: Name given to people who travel through time, either using a machine or under their own power, by exploiting possible loopholes in the laws of physics as we currently understand them.

Clone: A genetically identical copy of a human.

Cobots: Collaborative robots designed to work alongside human operators.

Concentrated Intelligence: An intelligent entity which has been spatially concentrated into a single, dense volume to reduce communications lag. Not as flexible as a distributed intelligence, but more efficient.

Continuity Identity Theory: The theory that "I" am the same person as various future and past selves with whom I am physically and temporally continuous.

Corpsicle: A slang term for a cryogenically preserved human who is awaiting revival by future technology.

Cryogenics: A branch of physics that studies materials at temperatures close to absolute zero.

Cryonaut: A person who has been cryonically suspended.

Cryonics: A branch of science aiming to develop a reversible suspended animation intended as a last resort for humans whose medical options have run out and who have the means to be frozen until a cure for their particular ailment becomes available.

Cryonic Suspension: A medical technique involving freezing to halt metabolic decay in order to prevent the permanent end-of-life in patients on the brink of death. The belief is that science will eventually advance to the point where revival of the person is possible.

Cyberspace: Originally coined by William Gibson in his 1984 novel *Neuromancer*, it refers to the totality of all the world's networked computers, often represented as a 3D virtual reality in which a person's actions have consequences in the real world.

Cyborg: From "cybernetic organism" is the term for a merging of human and machine where the technology is intended to enhance the human.

Dark Energy: A hypothetical form of energy that permeates the whole of space and is used to explain the accelerating expansion of the universe.

Dark Matter: A type of matter that hypothetically accounts for a large part of the total mass in the universe. As it cannot be seen directly and it neither emits nor absorbs light or other electromagnetic radiation, its existence is inferred from its gravitational effects on visible matter, radiation, and the large-scale structure of the universe.

Disassembler: The opposite of an Assembler, a machine or system of nanomachines that can take apart any object, a few atoms at a time, while recording its molecular structure. The results could then be studied or passed to an Assembler in order to make copies of the object.

Disrupter: Weapon that disintegrates its target by literally "disrupting" its molecular bonds. How this is achieved is never truly explained, but the two prevailing theories are via some kind of gravity beam that acts against the surrounding gravity, pulling the target apart or by using focused, high-frequency sound waves to shatter the target like a wine glass.

DNA (Deoxyribonucleic acid): The genetic coding, or instructions, used in the development and functioning of all known living things. Along with RNA and proteins, DNA is essential for all known forms of life.

Drake Equation: Named for Frank Drake, who came up with it in 1961 while at the National Astronomy and Ionosphere Center, it is a mathematical equation used to estimate the number of detectable extra-terrestrial civilisations in the Milky Way galaxy. It is still used today in the field of the Search for Extra-Terrestrial Intelligence (SETI).

Droid: Not much used outside of the *Star Wars* universe, it is a rough contraction of the word Android, but is used to refer to pretty much any kind of mechanised entity, whether intelligent or not.

Dryware: General science-fictional term for the artificial, machine-based parts of an android or cyborg.

Dying World: A little-used science-fiction subgenre in which an entire world reaches the end of its life, either through man-made depletion of resources or natural phenomena, and the physical laws of that world start to fail.

Dyson sphere: Named for physicist Freeman Dyson, it is the name given to a hypothetical "sphere" of orbiting satellites, built around a star, in order to harness its energy output. Dyson speculated that this kind of structure would be necessary to meet the escalating needs of a technologically advanced civilisation, and searching for existing structures of this kind could lead to the discovery of advanced intelligent life.

Dystopia: The opposite of a utopia, a dystopia is a society that in some way oppresses its people, usually through a totalitarian system of government that imposes extremely harsh punishments on anyone who transgresses the law, and is often characterised by a dehumanisation of its inhabitants. Although the underlying cause of the dystopia can vary enormously, popular depictions include problems with the environment, disease, depletion of natural resources, and lack of food, water, and basic medical care.

Empath: A person capable of reading the emotions of another through some form of telepathic or ESP ability. Different from a telepath, who can read thoughts and can be misled, an empath can detect the true emotions of a subject despite their outward demeanour.

ESP (Extra-Sensory Perception): No longer used in any scientific way, it is the generic term for what is often termed clairvoyance and includes telepathic and empathic abilities.

ET (ExtraTerrestrial): *See* Alien.

Ectogenesis (or In Vitro Reproduction): The growth of an organism in an artificial environment and outside of the body in which it would normally be found, such as the growth of an embryo or foetus in a synthetic womb, outside the mother's body.

EI (Emergent Intelligence): An intelligent system that gradually emerges bottom-up from simpler systems, instead of being designed top-down to be intelligent from the outset.

Emulation: An absolutely precise simulation of something, so exact that it is equivalent to the original.

Enhanced or Augmented Reality: A view of your real surroundings, usually through a screen or heads-up display of some kind, that has been enhanced or augmented with a set of personalised filters such as notes, descriptors, translations, and other information. Unlike Virtual Reality (VR), which is wholly immersive, simulated, and deals only with virtual objects, ER is designed to improve interaction with everyday objects, places, and situations.

First-contact: The term used for stories about the first meeting between human beings and other intelligent beings, generally those from other planets. First contact is generally made by humans exploring deep space who discover life on another planet or encounter another spaceship piloted by alien beings; occasionally however, intelligent beings do visit us here on Earth. These kind of stories almost always explore the same themes by holding a mirror up to ourselves and viewing our behaviour from the alien perspective.

Far Edge Party: Because exploring the star systems of the galaxy would take so long that most of the stars would die during the journey, one solution would be for the explorer to travel to a new system, replicate himself many times, and send each copy to a different system while he explores the current one. When the entire galaxy has been explored, the copies and the original all converge in one place and either swap or merge memories ("The Far Edge Party").

Femtotechnology: *See* Picotechnology.

Fermi's Paradox: Refers to the apparent contradiction between the probability of alien life existing, often calculated as quite high, and the total absence of any evidence for alien civilisations, or indeed alien life of any kind. Can be summed-up as *"If there are other intelligent beings in the Universe, why aren't they here?"*. Many explanations exist, such as the "Wildlife Preserve" idea (the aliens are keeping an eye on us but don't want to interfere) or that they are here but they are hidden from us, but none of them satisfy the problem.

Flatlander: Derogatory term for someone who has never ventured off a planetary surface into space.

Flying saucer: A round, flat object believed to be a spacecraft from another planet.

Forcefield: A hypothetical technology based on the manipulation of magnetic fields and usually deployed as an invisible shield around a spaceship or other craft as protection from attack.

Fourth dimension: Usually used to refer to time, the other three dimensions being length, width, and height.

FTL (Faster Than Light) Travel: A hypothetical means of breaking through the light speed barrier in order for a story to include easy and ubiquitous space travel. Examples of FTL travel proposals are the use of tachyons, the Alcubierre drive, and the traversable wormhole, although these solutions remain physically implausible at best.

Genie: Slang term for an AI that has been combined with an Assembler and that can build anything the owner wishes.

Goo/Grey Goo: Goo is the most common description of the by-product of millions of nanotech machines replicating uncontrollably as a kind of "cloud" that consumes, and thereby destroys, everything in its path. While unlikely, it is also the most often proposed disaster scenario involving the unchecked use of advanced nanotechnology. There are other kinds of Goo:

Blue Goo: Possibly named for law-enforcement use, refers to nano-machines used as protection against Grey Goo and other destructive nanomachines.

Green Goo: Nanomachines used by governments, corporations, or eco-terrorist groups for population control of humans or other creatures, possibly by sterilisation via otherwise harmless infections.

Golden Goo: A different kind of Grey Goo disaster whereby nano-machines filter gold from seawater. If this process got out of control we would get piles of Golden Goo at the expense of our seawater.

Khaki Goo: Grey Goo derived from military nanotechnology.

Pink Goo: Actually a sly dig at us humans, described as "...*apes who see their purpose as being fruitful and multiplying, filling up the cosmos with lots more such apes, unmodified.*"

Red Goo: The nanotechnology equivalent of a computer virus in that it is deliberately designed as destructive nanotechnology and released into the wild, as opposed to Grey Goo that is usually created accidentally.

Übergoo: A related term to Grey Goo that refers to the idea that during the singularity, powerful technologies would decimate non-transhumanists, which some transhumanists would find desirable.

Great Filter, The: The hypothetical mechanism by which potentially life-sustaining planets get filtered out before they can produce any intelligent life that can expand into cosmos.

Guy Fawkes Scenario: A theoretical scenario whereby unchecked availability and use of nanotechnology could conceivably allow anyone to commit a terrorist act (*see* Red Goo) such as constructing a large amount of explosives under a government building.

Generation ship: A classic science-fiction term for a very large vessel set up as a miniature ecology, in order to service an interstellar voyage in which many generations of crew live out the long transit time, as a self-sufficient society onboard.

Genetic engineering: A generic term for a combination of technologies used in the sophisticated manipulation of genetic material, whether animal, human, or alien, often producing uncontrollable chimeras.

Grok: A term lifted from Robert Heinlein's *Stranger In A Strange Land* (1959) which in Martian means, literally "to drink" but metaphorically means "to become one with," "know deeply," or "achieve unity with." At one time in vogue with 1960s U.S. counterculture it is still in common use on the Internet.

Habitat: The natural living environment of any species of animal, plant, or other type of organism, or the physical environment that surrounds, influences, and is utilised by a species population.

Hardware: A generic term for the various physical components that comprise a computer system, such as hard drive, motherboard, CPU, memory, etc.

Hive Computing: Making use of the spare capacity provided by unused computing resources in a network to speed up calculations or distribute parallel programs.

Hive Mind: A kind of group consciousness whereby all members of the group collectively share all the thoughts of the group, collecting, collating, analysing and disseminating information, and acting collectively according to a unified ideal response.

Humanoid: Any creature, biological or mechanical, designed to look like a human.

Hyperdrive: The common term for a stardrive.

Hyperspace: A common model for FTL travel in which a spaceship can exit normal space, enter a space where the light speed barrier does not apply, and then exit again at a chosen destination, allowing fast transit between two-points widely separated by normal space.

Implants: In science fiction an implant is usually either a man-made device designed and manufactured to enhance an existing biological structure or function, or a term used by UFO abductees to describe a physical object placed inside someone's body by aliens. Implants can also replace a missing biological structure, or support a damaged biological structure, or, as a microchip, contain a unique ID number that can be linked to a database containing information such as personal ID, medical history and conditions, criminal convictions, financial status and so on.

Infomorph: An intelligent Agent or information entity that has been uploaded to, and resides in, a computer or network.

Jump-drive: *See* Stardrive.

Jupiter-Brain: A post-human being, possibly augmented/constructed from nanomachines, that has developed vast computing power and size.

Laser: An acronym for Light Amplification by Stimulated Emission of Radiation, a laser is a device that emits light (electromagnetic radiation) through a process of optical amplification based on the stimulated emission of photons. Currently lasers could be used as weapons by causing either temporary or permanent loss of vision by being aimed directly at the eyes, but laser weapons capable of destroying a target during combat are still beyond the current technology in mobile power supply.

Lofstrom Loops: A Lofstrom or Launch Loop is an active structure, maglev, cable transport system, designed to achieve non-rocket space launch of vehicles by electromagnetically accelerating them so that they are projected into Earth orbit or even beyond. A working system could be suitable for repeated space tourism, space exploration, and space colonisation.

Magrifle: Short for magnetic rifle, a firearm similar to a rifle that uses pulsed magnetic fields rather than chemical explosives to propel projectiles.

Matter Transmission: Sometimes shortened to Transmat, is a term describing a theoretical technology that transports objects across distances by disassembling them at their transmission location, beaming the particles across space, and then reassembling them at the receiving location.

Megatechnology (or Megascale Engineering): Any technology that uses energies, scales or methods that are far beyond our current levels but still abide by the laws of physics, e.g. ground-to-orbit beanstalks, Lofstrom loops, terraforming, Dyson spheres, stellar husbandry, and Tipler cylinders.

Morphological Freedom: The ability to alter bodily form at will. This could be achieved through various technologies such as surgery, genetic engineering or nanotechnology.

Nanotechnology: Sometimes shortened to Nanotech, is the technology of manipulating matter on an atomic and molecular scale using tools, materials and other objects that are themselves of molecular scale, combining the autonomy and flexibility of living cells with the design and reliability of machines. Although currently a more-or-less hypothetical science, governments and corporations are nevertheless ploughing billions into nanotech research, implying as it does a world without material scarcity as any desired object can be easily and cheaply reproduced. It has spawned several related terms:

> **Nanarchist:** Someone who circumvents government control in order to use nanotechnology, or someone who advocates doing so.

> **Nanarchy:** The use of automatic law-enforcement by nanomachines that operate without human control.

> **Nanite:** A slang term for a nanomachine, in particular one that is able to self-replicate and/or self-repair. *See* Nanobot.

> **Nanobot:** A nano-scale robot, the essential machines that are used in nanotechnology.

> **Nanomachine:** *See* Nanobot.

> **Nanotech:** Shortened term, or slang for nanotechnology.

Neomorph: A transhuman or post-human with a non-humanoid body.

Omega Point: One possible future where the universe is under the total control of an intelligence, and the amount of information processed and stored converges towards infinity.

O'Neill Cylinders: Named for Gerard K. O'Neill, are pair of cylindrical space colonies that rotate around their respective axis, one clockwise, the other counterclockwise, to produce simulated gravity.

O'Neill Colony: A rotating space colony, especially large ones with internal ecosystems, such as O'Neill cylinders or Bernal spheres.

Orbital Tower: *See* Beanstalk.

Pattern Identity Theory: In the wake of cloning or post-humanism, the theory that "I" am the same individual as any other whose physical constitution forms the same or a similar pattern to mine.

Parallel Universe: A self-contained reality, separate and yet co-existing with our own.

Pharming: Short for pharmaceutical farming. The process of genetically engineering crops to protect them or their consumers from disease.

Pico Technology: Intended to parallel the term nanotechnology, this is a purely speculative technology that could manipulate matter on the pico-scale, three orders of magnitude smaller than nano-scale. Advancing on from this, the femto-scale would involve working with matter at the sub-atomic level.

Planets: A planet is an astronomical object, orbiting a star or stellar remnant, that is massive enough to be rounded by its own gravity, not so massive as to cause thermonuclear fusion, and has cleared its neighbouring region of planetary debris.

Plasma rifle: The long-barrelled version of a blaster, usually designed for longer-range use and a more destructive weapon with much higher energy requirements.

Post-Apocalyptic: Post-apocalyptic stories are a sub-genre of science fiction that deal with the impact on a world or civilisation of a catastrophic event such as nuclear warfare, global pandemic, impact event, climate change, exhaustion of natural resources, ecological collapse or alien invasion. Stories set in the immediate aftermath tend to focus on the psychology of survivors, those set much later often deal with remembrance of the old civilisation while building a new one. Generally in post-apocalyptic worlds, only scattered remnants of old technology remain.

Post-human: People of unlimited capacity; individuals with unprecedented physical, intellectual, and psychological capability who are self-programming, self-constituting and potentially immortal.

Pressor Beam: The opposite of a tractor beam, being a hypothetical device that can repel or repulse objects away from it.

Quantum Computing: A computer that makes direct use of quantum mechanical phenomena, such as superposition and entanglement, to perform operations on data. Quantum computers differ from digital computers because they do not require data to be encoded into bits, rather they use quantum properties to represent data and perform operations on these data.

Ray Gun: Whichever alternative name is used — ray gun, death ray, beam gun, blaster, laser gun, phaser, zap gun — they all function as guns on some level. A ray gun typically emits a visible ray that is lethal to a human target and will destroy a mechanical one.

Ringworld: A common science-fiction term that comes from Larry Niven's 1975 novel of the same name, it depicts a hoop, set around a star, that functions as an artificial macrostructure and home to a vast colony. Designed to provide an enormous surface area, life is supported on the inner surface where side walls hold in the atmosphere. Gravity comes from centrifugal force and day/night alternates via a ring of shadow squares orbiting separately closer to the star.

Regeneration tank: A complex nutrient bath that promotes healing in a damaged body and the regrowing of missing parts in a broken one. Usually depicted as a large fish tank in which the patient floats, unconscious, while the nutrients go to work.

Rejuvenation: A medical technology capable of reversing aging.

Robot: Derived from the Czech word *robota* meaning "involuntary worker" and first coined by Karel Capek in his 1920 play *Rossum's Universal Robots (R.U.R.)*, it refers to an electro-mechanical construct, usually humanoid in design and with humanlike capabilities, and very often depicted as mobile, self-aware, and free-thinking.

Sentient: A generic term referring to something other than a human, for example an extraterrestrial or alien, or a robot, android, or other mechanical or computing device, possessing a human-level intelligence to the degree that they can feel, perceive, or be conscious, and have subjective experiences.

Singularity: A supposed point in our future when the technology advances to such a degree that it brings about the emergence of a superintelligence. Since the capabilities of such intelligence are difficult for a human to comprehend, it is seen as an occurrence beyond which events cannot be predicted.

Skimmer: A type of vehicle, similar to a car, that works like a hovercraft, except that it uses some kind of antigravity propulsion rather than today's ducted fans.

Sky Hook: A cable, very similar to a beanstalk, that has been set in orbit around a planet but whose relative velocity at ground level is almost zero, allowing it to function like a space elevator.

Software: A collection of programs, procedures, algorithms, data, and documentation, held in storage on a computer, that tell the computer what to do and how to do it. Software is needed to control hardware.

Space: Space is the void that exists between stars, moons, and planets. It consists of a hard vacuum containing a plasma of hydrogen and helium, along with electromagnetic radiation, magnetic fields, and neutrinos.

Spacecraft (or Spaceship): A generic term for a craft designed to fly in outer space. It can be one of many kinds such as a freighter, cruiser, generation ship, troop transport, shuttle etc. but they are all, basically, spacecraft.

Space Elevator: A proposed type of space transportation system consisting of a cable or tether anchored to the Earth's surface and extending into space beyond geostationary orbit where the competing forces of gravity (from Earth) and centrifugal force (from the counterweight in space) would keep the cable under tension, and therefore stationary, over a single point on Earth. A vehicle could then theoretically travel up and down the cable, allowing entry into space without the use of rockets. *Also see* Beanstalk.

Space Fountain: Unlike a Space Elevator, a Space Fountain is a very tall tower that extends into space, but not to the height of geostationary orbit. However, as such a tower could not support its own weight, fast-moving pellets are shot up from the base of the tower and redirected back down once they reach the top, with the force of redirection holding the tower in place. A vehicle could then ascend/descend the tower by attaching itself to the pellets or simply climb the tower by some other means. While there are advantages to this concept — it requires less strength in its materials, can be built anywhere and doesn't need to be as high as a space elevator — the high power demands of the pellet system would be hugely expensive to run and loss of power could result in a catastrophic destruction of the tower.

Space opera: Based on the old westerns, these are at the same time the worst of science fiction and the best of science fiction; they are stories of the brave and bold, explorers opening up new frontiers, clearing the way for ordinary folk to follow on and build towns and start farms and begin mining and trading and all the other stuff that frontier towns have to do. There will be generally be "good guys" maintaining the law and "bad guys" in the shape of some enemy or another to be overcome, and all of this can happen in the farthest reaches of space or on a single newly colonised planet.

Spacesickness: Or microgravity nausea, is akin to motion sickness and is produced by confusion of the human vestibular system in the absence of a gravitational vertical. Interestingly space sickness was predicted in science fiction long before manned spaceflight, however NASA steadfastly avoids the term even today.

Stars: A star is a massive, luminous sphere of hydrogen and helium that has enough mass to sustain its own light and energy via thermonuclear fusion, which creates a tremendous amount of energy, causing the star to heat up and shine.

Stardrive: Also Hyperdrive, Jump Drive. A theoretical technology allowing FTL travel that can be built into individual spacecraft. There are a number of ideas on how a stardrive might work, but the most popular uses "jump points" in space — regions whose co-ordinates are mapped in such a way that instantaneous travel between them is possible using hyperspace. Common to this idea is the belief that a stardrive cannot be used within the gravity well of a planet, so spacecraft have to use a more conventional form of propulsion for launch and must reach near interstellar space before engaging the stardrive. It is also believed that the transition into and out of hyperspace causes enough stress and disorientation to humans that they become temporarily unable to function just after a jump.

Steampunk: A science-fiction sub-genre generally set in the Victorian or "Wild West" era where steam technology, in combination with clockwork or mechanical engines, is used to power everything from trains and carriages to tanks, dirigibles, assorted weaponry, and even robots. It has a very distinct design and manufacturing aesthetic with complex, often anachronistic, gadgets being fashioned from brass and leather and featuring delicate balances, glowing valves and intricately wrought engraving.

Stellar Husbandry: A hypothetical process through which a highly advanced civilisation could remove a substantial portion of a star's matter, in a controlled manner, to use for other purposes, for example power generation.

Stunner: Similar to Blaster or Ray Gun, Stunner is a common science-fiction name for a non-lethal, firearm-type weapon that renders the target unconscious, and victims often remain groggy, nauseated, and physically weak for a while after regaining consciousness.

Suspended Animation: A term that describes the theoretical ability to stop a biological system, usually human, through some form of immersion of extremely cold temperatures. It includes the ability to kick-start the biological system back into action at some point.

TAZ (Temporary Autonomous Zone): A transient location free of economic and/or social interference by the state.

Technocyte: A nanite, nanomachine, or other nanoscale device, introduced into the human bloodstream in order to effect repairs, protect against diseases such as cancer, act as an artificial immune system, or for a number of other uses.

Terraform: A very long-term project requiring megascale engineering to change the natural properties of a planet to make it more Earth-like. This could involve changing atmospheric composition, pressure, temperature, or the climate, and introducing a self-sustaining ecosystem in order that humans may colonise and live there independently.

Tipler Cylinder: Theoretical method of time-travel using the spacetime warping around a very massive, infinitely long cylinder, rotating near the speed of light around its axis.

Tractor Beam: The opposite of a pressor beam, is a hypothetical device, hugely popular in science fiction, that has the ability to attract an object towards it from some distance away. The most common use it as a kind of automated docking system to bring smaller, shuttle-type spacecraft into a larger ship.

Transhuman: Someone who is actively preparing to become post-human, who sees radical future possibilities in augmentation and takes every available option for self-enhancement.

Turing Test: Alan Turing's proposed test for whether a machine is conscious, or intelligent, or aware; a person communicates via text with it and with a hidden human, if they cannot tell which is which, we conclude that the computer is conscious.

Tachyons: Hypothetical subatomic particles that travel faster than light.

Telepath: A human or other being capable of directly reading the thoughts of others.

Teleport: The movement of an object from point-to-point without traversing the space in between. Similar to Matter Transmission.

Tellurian: *See* Terran.

Terran: A science-fictional adjective for anything whose origin is from Earth (Terra). A "Terran" is an Earth-descended human.

Time: Time, often referred to as the Fourth Dimension, the others being width, height and length, is the dimension in which events can be ordered from the past through the present into the future, and also the measure of durations of events and the intervals between them.

Timeline: A timeline is a simple way of displaying a list of events in chronological order, and is often used in research to help understand events or trends for a particular topic. In science-fiction, it can mean any single universe in a set of branching histories, implying that travel across timelines is possible, even if time travel between different points on the same timeline is not.

Time Machine: A machine that can carry people backwards and forwards along timelines.

Time Warp: A theoretical irregularity in a timeline, creating a break or point at which people and things can move between different times.

Tractor beam: The opposite of a Pressor Beam, a generic science fiction term for a device that can lock onto an object and pull the objects towards itself.

Transmat: *See* Matter Transmission.

Trekker: A hardcore fan of the television programme *Star Trek*.

Ubiquitous Computing: A way of describing computers as an integral, invisible part of every aspect of people's lives, with computers adapting seamlessly to human behaviour rather than requiring humans to change their behaviours to adapt to the computer.

UFO (Unidentified Flying Object): A generic term for any strange object that flies through the sky that no one can identify. Usually attributed to supposed alien spacecraft, and used as an indicator of life on other planets, but could equally be a prototype aircraft being tested in secret.

Utopia: An ideal society. A community that is generally free of things like hunger, disease, and conflict, where the inhabitants have a large degree of leisure time, and the way of life is regarded as perfect. In science fiction it is generally discovered that any utopia is, under the surface, actually a dystopia for at least some of the people. In both cases the prevailing issues are of loss of freedom and loss of control over one's own life.

Virtual Reality (VR): A computer-generated environment that can simulate physical presence in places in the real world or in an imaginary world. VR is wholly immersive, requiring the user to wear a stereoscopic headset and haptic gloves in order to experience the sights, sounds, and tactile information being generated.

Virtual Community: A community of persons based in disparate locations who have formed a cultural community via a computer network.

von Neumann Machine: A self-replicating machine, often proposed as a cheap way to colonise an entire solar system or galaxy, as it is able to build working copies of itself using only materials found in its environment.

Warpdrive: *See* Stardrive.

Wetware: *See also* Dryware. Similar to hardware, although generally refers to the biological parts of a biotech or cybernetic system. In a Cyborg this would most commonly be the human nervous system.

Waldo: A Waldo is a generic term in science fiction for a remote mechanical arm or hand that duplicates the movements of a human operator. Although this term has been around for a long time, The Character Shop, an animatronic and puppet-effects company in Simi Valley, California, has actually trademarked the term.

Wormhole: More properly known in physics as an Einstein-Rosen Bridge, a wormhole is a hypothetical topological feature that, essentially, acts as a "short cut" between two points in spacetime. To imagine a wormhole, picture a piece of paper with a dot at either end. To travel between the two dots would take time, but if you could fold the paper over so that the two dots meet, and then travel through a hole in the paper from one dot to the other, your travel time would be instantaneous. If they existed, or could be built, wormholes would provide a way to travel at FTL speeds.

Xenobiology: The study of alien life forms and their biology.

ABOUT THE AUTHOR

ROBERT GRANT is a writer, screenwriter, and script consultant based in London, England, with a penchant for science fiction and fantasy. He sits on the jury of the Arthur C. Clarke Award for Science Fiction Literature, the most prestigious science fiction award the UK has to offer, and he is one of the core team behind The London International Festival of Science Fiction and Fantastic Film (or SCI-FI-LONDON, as they like to be known).

Robert runs the workshops and panels that make up the filmmaking and literary strands of the festival, as well as being Literary Editor at sci-fi-london.com. As a result, he watches and reads far more science fiction in a year than can possibly be good for him.

When he's not telling tall tales or spinning short stories he designs user-interfaces for things, lusts after the latest filmmaking technology, quietly obsesses over good design and bemoans the lot of his beloved Liverpool Football Club.

He can be found lurking @swinefever.

SAVE THE CAT!®
THE LAST BOOK ON SCREENWRITING YOU'LL EVER NEED!

BLAKE SNYDER

BEST SELLER

He made millions of dollars selling screenplays to Hollywood and here screenwriter Blake Snyder tells all. "Save the Cat!®" is just one of Snyder's many ironclad rules for making your ideas more marketable and your script more satisfying — and saleable, including:

- The four elements of every winning logline.
- The seven immutable laws of screenplay physics.
- The 10 genres and why they're important to your movie.
- Why your Hero must serve your idea.
- Mastering the Beats.
- Mastering the Board to create the Perfect Beast.
- How to get back on track with ironclad and proven rules for script repair.

This ultimate insider's guide reveals the secrets that none dare admit, told by a show biz veteran who's proven that you can sell your script if you can save the cat.

"Imagine what would happen in a town where more writers approached screenwriting the way Blake suggests? My weekend read would dramatically improve, both in sellable/producible content and in discovering new writers who understand the craft of storytelling and can be hired on assignment for ideas we already have in house."
> – From the Foreword by Sheila Hanahan Taylor, Vice President, Development at Zide/Perry Entertainment, whose films include *American Pie, Cats and Dogs, Final Destination*

"One of the most comprehensive and insightful how-to's out there. Save the Cat!® is a must-read for both the novice and the professional screenwriter."
> – Todd Black, Producer, *The Pursuit of Happyness, The Weather Man, S.W.A.T, Alex and Emma, Antwone Fisher*

"Want to know how to be a successful writer in Hollywood? The answers are here. Blake Snyder has written an insider's book that's informative — and funny, too."
> – David Hoberman, Producer, *The Shaggy Dog* (2005), *Raising Helen, Walking Tall, Bringing Down the House, Monk* (TV)

BLAKE SNYDER, besides selling million-dollar scripts to both Disney and Spielberg, was one of Hollywood's most successful spec screenwriters. Blake's vision continues on *www.blakesnyder.com.*

$19.95 · 216 PAGES · ORDER NUMBER 34RLS · ISBN: 9781932907001

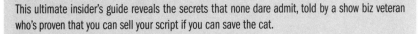

THE WRITER'S JOURNEY - 3RD EDITION
MYTHIC STRUCTURE FOR WRITERS

CHRISTOPHER VOGLER

BEST SELLER

See why this book has become an international best seller and a true classic. *The Writer's Journey* explores the powerful relationship between mythology and storytelling in a clear, concise style that's made it required reading for movie executives, screenwriters, playwrights, scholars, and fans of pop culture all over the world.

Both fiction and nonfiction writers will discover a set of useful myth-inspired storytelling paradigms (i.e., "The Hero's Journey") and step-by-step guidelines to plot and character development. Based on the work of Joseph Campbell, *The Writer's Journey* is a must for all writers interested in further developing their craft.

The updated and revised third edition provides new insights and observations from Vogler's ongoing work on mythology's influence on stories, movies, and man himself.

"This book is like having the smartest person in the story meeting come home with you and whisper what to do in your ear as you write a screenplay. Insight for insight, step for step, Chris Vogler takes us through the process of connecting theme to story and making a script come alive."
>   – Lynda Obst, producer, *Sleepless in Seattle, How to Lose a Guy in 10 Days*;
>   author, *Hello, He Lied*

"This is a book about the stories we write, and perhaps more importantly, the stories we live. It is the most influential work I have yet encountered on the art, nature, and the very purpose of storytelling."
>   – Bruce Joel Rubin, screenwriter, *Stuart Little 2, Deep Impact,*
>   *Ghost, Jacob's Ladder*

CHRISTOPHER VOGLER is a veteran story consultant for major Hollywood film companies and a respected teacher of filmmakers and writers around the globe. He has influenced the stories of movies from *The Lion King* to *Fight Club* to *The Thin Red Line* and most recently wrote the first installment of *Ravenskull*, a Japanese-style manga or graphic novel. He is the executive producer of the feature film *P.S. Your Cat is Dead* and writer of the animated feature *Jester Till*.

$26.95 · 448 PAGES · ORDER NUMBER 76RLS · ISBN: 9781932907360

THE MYTH OF MWP

In a dark time, a light bringer came along, leading the curious and the frustrated to clarity and empowerment. It took the well-guarded secrets out of the hands of the few and made them available to all. It spread a spirit of openness and creative freedom, and built a storehouse of knowledge dedicated to the betterment of the arts.

The essence of the Michael Wiese Productions (MWP) is empowering people who have the burning desire to express themselves creatively. We help them realize their dreams by putting the tools in their hands. We demystify the sometimes secretive worlds of screenwriting, directing, acting, producing, film financing, and other media crafts.

By doing so, we hope to bring forth a realization of 'conscious media' which we define as being positively charged, emphasizing hope and affirming positive values like trust, cooperation, self-empowerment, freedom, and love. Grounded in the deep roots of myth, it aims to be healing both for those who make the art and those who encounter it. It hopes to be transformative for people, opening doors to new possibilities and pulling back veils to reveal hidden worlds.

MWP has built a storehouse of knowledge unequaled in the world, for no other publisher has so many titles on the media arts. Please visit www.mwp.com where you will find many free resources and a 25% discount on our books. Sign up and become part of the wider creative community!

Onward and upward,

Michael Wiese
Publisher/Filmmaker